Emulation Working Today

Emulation Working Today

by

G.F. Redman

P.G.Swd.B.

Assistant Grand Secretary

(Member of the Committee of Emulation Lodge of
Improvement 1980–; Senior Member 2002–)

To VW Bro. Hayden Sharp, P.G.Swd.B.

My predecessor as Senior Member of the
Committee of Emulation Lodge of Improvement

First published 2007

ISBN (10): 0 85318 276 0
ISBN (13): 978 0 85318 276 4

© G.F. Redman 2007

Published by Lewis Masonic

an imprint of Ian Allan Publishing Ltd,
Hersham, Surrey KT12 4RG.
Printed by Ian Allan Printing Ltd,
Hersham, Surrey KT12 4RG

Code: 0711/

Contents

Dedication   iv
Foreword   vii
Preface   ix

Part I

Chapter 1 – Emulation Lodge of Improvement   3
Chapter 2 – The Purpose of this Book   10

Part II

Chapter 3 – General Remarks   17
Chapter 4 – The Tyler   24
Chapter 5 – The Inner Guard   28
Chapter 6 – The Deacons   36
Chapter 7 – The Junior Deacon   46
Chapter 8 – The Senior Deacon   54
Chapter 9 – The Secretary   62
Chapter 10– The Treasurer   65
Chapter 11– The Wardens   66
Chapter 12– The Junior Warden   71
Chapter 13– The Senior Warden   74
Chapter 14– The Master Elect   76
Chapter 15– The Worshipful Master   79
Chapter 16– The Installing Master   102
Chapter 17– The Immediate Past Master   119
Chapter 18– The Lectures   124
Chapter 19– Emulation Procedures   131

Part III

Chapter 20 – The Chaplain   141
Chapter 21 – The Director of Ceremonies   143
Chapter 22 – The Almoner   151
Chapter 23 – The Charity Steward   152
Chapter 24 – The Assistant Director of Ceremonies   153
Chapter 25 – The Organist   154
Chapter 26 – The Assistant Secretary   156
Chapter 27 – The Stewards   157

Appendices

Appendix 1 – A Few Words...   158
Appendix 2 – The Immortal Memory...   161

Foreword

Grand Lodge has always been careful not to give its formal approval to any one version of the English Craft ritual. But I am sure that of the many versions that exist Emulation Working is the most widely used, and for many of us it provides a point of reference to which we can turn when the need arises.

Few of us reach 'silver matchbox' standard in the ceremonies that we work, but I hope that every Freemason who takes office in a Lodge strives to perform his ritual work to the best of his ability. This book by Brother Graham Redman will certainly be of immense help to anyone who wishes to work the Emulation Ritual exactly 'according to the book', but it also includes many helpful hints about adapting the strict requirements of the Emulation Ritual to situations which can arise in an ordinary Lodge. Few, if any, Brethren can be better qualified to give guidance on Emulation Working than Brother Redman, who has been a member of the precepting Committee of Emulation Lodge of Improvement for over a quarter of a century.

Northampton
Pro Grand Master

Preface

I started to write this book towards the very end of 1986, not long after the Grand Lodge had passed its historic resolution to remove the penalties from the obligations in the three degrees and the Installation and transfer them to other parts of the respective ceremonies. Emulation Lodge of Improvement had, in common with the other ritual bodies, settled the necessary revisions to the Ritual Book, and Lodges were starting to adjust to the new wording.

It was then nearer sixty years than fifty since W Bro. H.F. Inman's "Emulation-Working Explained" was first published. In the intervening years there had been several publications intended to give still greater guidance on the correct method of working the ceremonies of Craft Freemasonry according to the system demonstrated in the Emulation Lodge of Improvement, of which the latest was the official Emulation Ritual, first published in 1969, and then in its eighth (now in its twelfth) edition.

By March, 1987 I had written the first draft of most of what now forms Part II of this book, and had submitted a synopsis and second draft of some pilot chapters to A Lewis (Masonic Publishing) Limited, which expressed interest in publishing it. A consultancy which covered most of the middle part of that year slowed my work on the project considerably, and when I joined the Grand Secretary's staff in November, 1987 I found that the pressures of assimilating my new duties militated against further progress in the immediate future. After some further desultory discussions with the publishers, work stopped completely and the book went into limbo.

There it remained until the spring of 2006, when I had a meeting (on unrelated matters) in the week of the Annual Investiture with several senior Brethren from the District of Natal who were in London for the Craft and Royal Arch Investitures. W Bro. Douglas Kirton, one of the Assistant District Grand Masters and a former District Grand Director of Ceremonies, asked me at one point when Inman's book was going to be republished. I replied that it was unlikely that it would ever be, but that I had done some work many years previously on a book that would cover broadly the same ground.

It so happened that in the summer of 2005 I had mentioned the book to W Bro. David Allan of the Ian Allan Group which had for many years owned A Lewis (Masonic Publishing) Limited, and he had expressed interest in it. Within a week or two of my meeting with the Natal Brethren I had dug out the typescript of the synopsis and pilot chapters and sent them to him. The response I received was still favourable, but I had the practical difficulty of finding time to revise the chapters that were already written and write those that still remained to be done, as a temporary vacancy in the office of Grand Secretary had caused a significant increase in my duties at Freemasons' Hall.

In the result I restarted the task late in 2006, almost exactly twenty years after I first began to write. Fortunately, I had periodically converted the computer files in which the various chapters were stored, as successive word processor programs became obsolete, so that I still had the text available in electronic format; transferring these to my Psion palmtop made it possible for me to make full use of odd moments of spare time in order to carry out the revision of the existing text and the writing of the new chapters. Now, in the spring of 2007, the work is at last completed.

* * *

There are countless Brethren whom I might thank, for any author of a "how to..." book is bound to be indebted to those from whom he himself learnt how. I hope I may be forgiven for those whom I fail to thank by name, but time and space (as well as my memory) preclude me from naming all of them. Principally, I have to thank the many preceptors who formally or informally gave me the benefit of their experience during the early part of my Masonic career; amongst these (though in a rather different league) are the Brethren who have been members of the Committee of Emulation Lodge of Improvement during the time since I joined it early in 1974, many of whom are no longer alive to be thanked in person. I must, however, make specific mention of my four particular mentors on the Emulation Committee: VW Bro. Hayden Sharp, who was my immediate predecessor as Senior Member of the Committee (to whom this book is dedicated), the late RW Bro. Judge Alan Trapnell, another former Senior Member, and the late W Bros. Colin Dyer and Reginald Marley.

For reasons that will be obvious, it would be remiss of me not to mention W Bro. Douglas Kirton, without whose fortuitous enquiry this book would probably never have been completed or published. Last, and by no means least, I wish to thank MW Bro. Lord Northampton, Pro Grand Master, for agreeing to contribute a Foreword to this work.

Graham Redman
April, 2007

PART I

Chapter 1

Emulation Lodge of Improvement

Brief History

It is now almost two hundred years since the Lodge of Reconciliation was set up in early December, 1813, just before the union of the two rival Grand Lodges on 27th December of that year, to settle, and afterwards to demonstrate, the form of the ritual for the United Grand Lodge of England. The Lodge of Reconciliation ceased working in June, 1816 after the new ritual had been approved at the Quarterly Communication of the Grand Lodge. The Stability Lodge of Instruction, which included several members of the Lodge of Reconciliation amongst its leaders, started working in 1817, but Emulation Lodge of Improvement was not founded until October, 1823. Emulation can, however, claim indirectly almost as close a connection with the Lodge of Reconciliation as can Stability, because many of the Founders of Emulation Lodge of Improvement had been members of the Burlington and the Perseverance Lodges of Instruction. Burlington started working in 1810 (under the Premier or "Moderns" Grand Lodge) and Perseverance started in 1818. There was a substantial degree of common membership as well as a certain amount of "in and out running" between the two, so that although Burlington was in abeyance for two relatively short periods, the net result was a virtually unbroken line of succession, from the time that the Lodge of Reconciliation settled and demonstrated the ritual of the three degrees, down to the foundation of Emulation.

It was on 2nd October, 1823 that the Emulation Lodge of Improvement for Master Masons first met under the sanction of the Lodge of Hope, No. 7 (in 1832 renamed Royal York Lodge of Perseverance, No. 7). When it started working, Emulation taught the ritual settled by the Lodge of

Reconciliation by means of the Lectures, and did not begin regularly to demonstrate the actual ceremonies until some time – the exact date is uncertain – in the 1830s. The Lectures were in those days the normal method of teaching the ritual, and Emulation from the beginning worked the Lectures according to The Grand Stewards' Lodge system, which incorporated the new ritual from 1815; The Grand Stewards' Lodge continued to demonstrate its Lectures at its twice-yearly Public Nights until the latter ceased to be held after 1867. Emulation adhered to that system, incorporated changes as they were introduced by The Grand Stewards' Lodge and, most important, has continued to work them regularly up to the present day.

It was not long before the future of the newly established Lodge of Improvement seemed to be under serious threat. From 1818, the Book of Constitutions provided (as it still does) that every Lodge of Instruction had to be held either under the sanction of a regular Lodge, or by the licence and authority of the Grand Master. Although from 1823, Emulation was sponsored by the Lodge of Hope, in March, 1830 it seemed likely that, following a message sent by the Grand Master, the Duke of Sussex, to the Quarterly Communication of Grand Lodge held at the beginning of the month, the Rules in the Book of Constitutions would be tightened to require the Master or a Past Master of the sanctioning Lodge in future to preside at every meeting of a Lodge of Instruction. At this time the Lodge of Hope was very small, and rather weak. The members of Emulation present at the meeting on 19th March decided to protect their position by submitting a Memorial to the Grand Master, reciting their special circumstances as a general Lodge of Instruction serving many Lodges and not just the sanctioning Lodge, and praying the Grand Master to grant them his special licence for the future.

The Grand Master, through the Grand Secretary, declined to grant such a licence, and the members of Emulation therefore felt it prudent to seek sanction from a stronger Lodge. They chose the Lodge of Unions, to which several members of Emulation then belonged and which has remained the sponsoring Lodge to this day.

Emulation has over the years enjoyed the support of not only many distinguished, but also many dedicated, Freemasons. Among the distinguished have been four Grand Secretaries, three Presidents of the Board of General Purposes, five Grand Directors of Ceremonies and several Provincial Grand Masters. The first of the dedicated was Bro. Peter Gilkes, who joining Emulation in 1825 rapidly became its acknowledged leader till his death in December 1833; it was he who gave Emulation its abiding ethos of always checking the passing error lest it should pass into common currency.

This book is intended as a guide to the ritual and it would therefore be out of place to dwell at length on the history of Emulation Lodge of Improvement. The reader who wishes to know more of its history can do no better than to read the late Bro. Colin Dyer's excellent history, "Emulation: a Ritual to Remember" which he wrote for Emulation's Sesquicentenary in 1973.

The Emulation Ritual

For many years the Committee refused to give the Emulation *imprimatur* to a published ritual, with the result that a number of ritual books purporting to reflect Emulation working came into existence. Ultimately the most widely used of these was the "Nigerian Ritual" which was published by A Lewis just before the Second World War; it was notable for containing far more explicit rubrics than any ritual book that had gone before, and probably if the War had not concentrated minds and efforts elsewhere, attempts might have been made to suppress it. By the time normality returned after the War the "Nigerian Ritual", which had proved immensely popular with Brethren, had gained too firm a hold for suppression to be a viable option. Eventually it seemed to the Committee that nothing was to be gained by refusing any longer to authorise an official version, and in 1969 the Emulation Ritual was published. Agreement was reached with A Lewis for the publication of the new work, it being a part of the agreement that the publisher would withdraw from sale its other Emulation rituals, such as the Perfect Ceremonies and the Nigerian Ritual.

While it would be presumptuous to claim that Emulation has preserved every word of the 1816 ritual unchanged over the intervening years, successive members of the precepting Committee have ensured that, as far as possible, no changes have crept in through inadvertence. The Committee has, indeed, maintained over the years that it has no authority to vary the ritual that was settled by the Grand Lodge in 1816, and has therefore only made changes in the wording of the ceremonies in response to resolutions of Grand Lodge. Both Grand Lodge, however, and its Board of General Purposes have been notably reluctant to become involved in pronouncing on the detail of Masonic ritual, with the result that the only significant changes formally authorised have involved the penalties. In 1964, the Provincial Grand Master for Norfolk, Bishop Herbert, moved a resolution in Grand Lodge authorising the use of a formula ("ever bearing in mind the traditional penalty on the violation of any of them, that of having the . . . ") which made it plain that the penalties in the Obligations were figurative merely – the so-called "permissive variations", which Emulation demonstrated on the second Friday in each month from 1965 until 1986.

There seems little doubt that many senior Freemasons had hoped that the permissive variations would gain wide currency and eventually supplant the older form of the penalties. In the event, however, Lodges showed no sign of a rapid shift to the newer form and in 1985 the Board of General Purposes returned to the issue. A more extensive revision of the ceremonies was undertaken, removing the penalties from the obligations and transferring them to other parts of the ritual. A number of demonstrations of the revised ritual were given to Provincial Grand Masters and in Installed Masters Lodges, in London and elsewhere, during the autumn of 1985 and the early part of 1986, with a view to informing Masonic opinion. The changes were debated in Grand Lodge at the Quarterly Communication in June, 1986 and were approved by a substantial majority, though to the regret of many. Lodges were given a period of grace before they were obliged to adopt the new forms, and in the meantime the various ritual bodies, including Emulation, had the task of revising their rituals to incorporate the changes Grand Lodge had made.

The result was a new "Revised Edition", which achieved a very heavy sale as Brethren familiarised themselves with the new wordings.

The Silver Matchbox

On 22nd October, 1897 Bro. Major R.L.S. Badham, who was occupying the Chair, worked the second degree in a manner described as exemplary by the then Senior Member of the Committee, Bro. Robert Clay Sudlow, who was precepting on that occasion. Sudlow subsequently presented him with a silver matchbox to mark the achievement; he also – at his own expense until the rest of the Committee decided that he should be relieved of the burden – made similar presentations to other Brethren attaining a similar standard. Within a few years it had become the established custom, and a Brother who works a ceremony from the Chair "without standing in need of prompting or correction" receives a silver matchbox, engraved on the front with his name and on the reverse with the heading "E. L. OF I." and beneath it the ceremony he has worked, together with the year (e.g. "2ND. DEG. & T.B. 1975"). If the Brother subsequently works a different ceremony without correction, that is recorded in the same fashion, and if he has worked all four ceremonies without correction, the words "COMPLETE RECORD" are added at the foot of the list. In order to qualify, the ceremony must be worked by the Master without *any* mistakes in either words or actions.

As at the end of April, 2007 345 Brethren have received a matchbox, of whom 120 have achieved a complete record.

There is no doubt that over the years many Brethren have been inspired to work at Emulation Lodge of Improvement by the prospect of winning this unusual accolade. It should not, however, be overlooked that a matchbox is an indication only of strict accuracy; it says nothing about the quality or impressiveness of the ceremony. Many word-perfect ceremonies can only be described as pedestrian, while conversely many Brethren whom the matchbox has eluded to the end of their days at Emulation have worked inspirational ceremonies of which anyone could be justly proud.

Recognised Lodges of Instruction

Early in the twentieth century a system of recognised Lodges of Instruction began. The Committee of Emulation Lodge of Improvement approves Preceptors as teaching the ritual in strict accordance with Emulation working, and this confers recognition on the Lodge of Instruction concerned. A Brother who aspires to work in the Chair at Emulation must normally have a "chit" from an approved Preceptor to certify that he is capable of doing the work to the required standard.

Each year in June at the annual Preceptors' Festival, all the offices are filled by Brethren from recognised Lodges of Instruction, who demonstrate one of the three degrees (in rotation), followed by the Ceremony of Installation. This is therefore, in effect, a scratch team, many of the members of which will be strangers to the others, and it shows that it is possible for Brethren who have been trained in Emulation working in different parts of the country to come together and work successfully.

Emulation Today

Emulation Lodge of Improvement meets at Freemasons' Hall, Great Queen Street, London, every Friday from October to June inclusive, except over the Christmas and New Year break and Good Friday. Meetings begin at 6.15 p.m., except for the Annual Festival which is held on the last Friday in February (5.30 p.m.) and the Preceptors' Festival on the last Friday in June (4.30 p.m.). The Brethren dine together only after the two Festivals.

Brethren attending for the first time, unless vouched for in person by a known Brother, must be prepared to be proved in all the signs, Tns. and words of the three degrees. Except at the Festivals, where ordinary undress regalia is worn (without gloves) as at a normal Lodge meeting, the dress code is "smart casual", with a Master Mason's or Installed Master's apron, as the case may be, apart from the members of the Committee, who wear the aprons of their respective ranks, but without collars.

At the first meeting of the season, when the Chair is taken by a member of the Committee (generally one who is trying to complete his record for the matchbox), and the last, which is the Preceptors' Festival, the programme consists of one of the three degrees in the first part of the evening, and the ceremony of Installation in the second. At the Annual Festival, four Lecture Sections are worked by members of the Committee assisted by Brethren who have shown special ability in the ritual. At the remaining meetings, the first part of the evening is taken up by one of the four ceremonies, worked in rotation, and the second part by a section from one of the Lectures.

It would be idle to pretend that Emulation is today anything like the force it was in former times. The late Bro. Colin Dyer, in his history already referred to, expressed the view in 1973 that the use of detailed books of ritual seemed to have taken the place temporarily of the comradeship of the Lodge of Instruction, but hoped that falling numbers might prove to be a passing phase. That assessment now appears to have been unduly optimistic. Lodges of Instruction generally are in serious decline, and Emulation with them. This is the result of social and other pressures which in recent years have militated against regular weekly attendance, and there is no sign at present of those pressures abating. Nevertheless, Emulation still teaches and maintains the highest standards of Masonic ritual, and though there are nowadays fewer of them, the best workers today are still as good as the best in earlier days. So long as there remains a demand, Emulation will continue to meet it.

Chapter 2

The Purpose of this Book

This book sets out to provide as accurate as possible a description of Emulation working – that is the Craft ritual, and the manner of working it, which is demonstrated in Emulation Lodge of Improvement each Friday throughout nine months of every year. In practice there can hardly be a single Lodge that works the ritual in every detail exactly as it is demonstrated in Emulation Lodge of Improvement; nevertheless, more Lodges under the English Constitution use Emulation working as the basis of their ceremonies than any other, even though they may have incorporated – by accident or design – their own particular variations.

This is not intended as a book to stand alone. It is intended as a supplement to the Emulation Ritual book and in part as a commentary on it. It does not claim to be exhaustive as a description of Emulation working, for in many, if not most, cases the Emulation Ritual is quite clear as to the procedure that is to be followed. There are, however, many instances where, despite what might be thought a clear description in the rubric of the Ritual, Brethren commonly fail to carry out the work in accordance with Emulation working, which, it should not be forgotten, preserves as far as possible the only Craft ritual that has ever been formally approved by the Grand Lodge. There can be various reasons for such failures: sometimes a weak or ignorant Director of Ceremonies or Preceptor may have allowed Brethren to fall into careless habits; conversely a strong Director of Ceremonies or Preceptor may have enforced his idiosyncratic views; whichever may be the case, that fickle and shifting concept, the tradition of the Lodge, is usually invoked as justification. Leaving aside such shortcomings in the ritual actions, there are also several "accident black spots" where the wording of the ritual is liable regularly to be rendered inaccurately.

This book therefore sets out, first, to provide a second bearing where difficulties are known to arise, rather like the geometric principle which enables a surveyor or cartographer to pinpoint a spot by the process of triangulation. It is to be hoped that the alternative descriptions provided in this book will render clearer those procedures which most often defeat Brethren. Secondly, by warning of the "black spots" and providing mnemonics or other strategies to help pass through them safely, this book is aimed at making the task of the various Officers of a Lodge easier.

This book is intended to operate on various levels. On one level it is a guide for those Brethren who aspire to work at Emulation Lodge of Improvement – and perhaps gain a silver matchbox. On another level it is a handbook for preceptors of Lodges of Instruction, whether Emulation-recognised or not, as well as for the Directors of Ceremonies who have, often on the afternoon of the meeting itself, to put through their paces the Brethren of those Lodges (all too numerous these days) that have no Lodge of Instruction attached. Most of all, however, it is intended as a guide for the Brethren of ordinary Lodges while they are working their way up to the Chair and even after, when they may find themselves appointed or elected to one of the "permanent" offices.

A word first as to the layout of this book. While it is far from being an updated version of W Bro. H.F. Inman's "Emulation-Working Explained", despite a certain similarity in title, I have found it impossible to avoid being influenced, at least in part, by what has gone before. Therefore I have found Inman's method of dealing with each Officer and his duties in turn to be a helpful one. On the other hand I am also endeavouring to reflect the ritual practice of Emulation Lodge of Improvement, where only certain of the Officers whom a Master may appoint actually have a part to play in the ceremonies. For this reason I have divided this book into three parts. The first, of which this chapter is part, consists of introductory material. The second deals with the Officers and their duties when the Emulation system is followed without deviation, that is the duties of the regular Officers of a Lodge as provided for in Rule 104(a) of the Book of Constitutions; it also contains a chapter on the Lectures of Craft Masonry and a chapter on the procedures adopted in Emulation Lodge of Improvement at its regular meetings. The third part deals with the ceremonial duties of the additional Officers also provided for in Rule 104(a) where, as is the almost invariable custom, a Lodge wishes to appoint them. Each chapter is, generally, itself divided into two parts, the first dealing with ritual – on which alone Emulation holds itself out as an authority – the second with procedure, where the practice of Emulation may be useful as a guide. Finally, I have added two short appendices, covering respectively problems of pronunciation, and techniques for memorising and remembering the ritual.

Bro. Inman, in his book, displayed a tendency to intersperse directions on ritual with those on procedure, and to leaven the mixture thereby obtained with a number of expressions of his own opinion, so that the reader unfamiliar with the practice of the Emulation Lodge of Improvement might have been forgiven for attributing to Emulation a degree of arrogance in certain matters over which it has never claimed to possess any authority. Few authors can resist the temptation at times to present their own private opinions to their readers, and I do not claim to be an exception to the general rule. I have tried, however, as far as practicable, to keep the chapters in the second part factual and descriptive, though I have found it impossible to avoid occasionally expressing my own views on matters that some might regard as mildly controversial. In the third part, where I have of necessity moved away from the strict scheme of Emulation, I have once or twice "spread myself" and expressed more controversial views. I hope, however, that by adopting the layout that I have chosen, I will leave the reader in no doubt where the line between firmly established Emulation practice and my personal opinion is to be drawn.

I offer one final observation, which is rather an obvious one: the greater amount of detail now shown in the rubrics of the ritual has undoubtedly encouraged Brethren in the view that there is no longer any need to attend a Lodge of Instruction in order to learn the correct method of working. While it is eminently possible – and it is, indeed, the easiest way – to learn the words of the ritual from a book, the actions are a different matter. For them there is ultimately no substitute for the kind of experience to be gained in a Lodge of Instruction. This book will take a Brother part – perhaps even most – of the way but it is not the same as receiving instruction at first hand from a competent preceptor or attending a Lodge of demonstration such as Emulation Lodge of Improvement.

PART II

Chapter 3

General Remarks

The succeeding chapters in this section deal with the duties of the individual Officers of a Lodge. But of course every Brother has a certain minimum of ritual actions to perform, even if it is only to stand to order during the opening and closing of the Lodge. Similarly, certain actions are common to all the Officers of a Lodge. This chapter, therefore, deals with various basic matters, both for the guidance of Brethren who are not in office, and so as to avoid repetition when the duties of the individual Officers are considered separately.

Before going any further, it will be helpful if I draw some distinctions. One commonly drawn in this book is between ritual and procedure. By ritual, I mean the form of words and the accompanying actions used in the various ceremonies which are set out in the published Emulation Ritual; by procedure, I mean the other items of business carried on at any Lodge meeting, for which no form is laid down in the published ritual, but which by their very nature inevitably need to be carried out with a measure of formality. There is another distinction, rarely used in this book, between ritual and ceremonial. In this sense, ritual means the spoken word; whereas ceremonial means the actions which accompany those words, or which stand by themselves. The word "ceremony" can also be used in contrast to procedure, to cover a complete set of words and actions – e.g. the ceremony of Initiation, or the ceremony of opening the Lodge in the third degree – contained in the published Ritual. And there is a yet further meaning for ceremonial – to describe major events generally conducted under the auspices of Grand Lodge or a Metropolitan, Provincial or District Grand Lodge.

The most basic matter is that of the signs in the three degrees. Signs are given when the Master or some other Officer directs; during the obligations; and when addressing a superior Officer. At no time during the ceremonies as carried out in Emulation Lodge of Improvement, and only rarely during the Lectures or items of procedure, does an Officer stand to order when an exchange is *originated* by the Master or a superior Officer. The best illustration of this point is the ceremony of opening the Lodge in the second or third degree. When the Master addresses the Junior Warden, and the Junior Warden addresses the Inner Guard, the junior Officer does not stand to order. But a few moments later when he reports back to his superior, each does take a step and give the sign, because it is he who is initiating the exchange.

In almost every case, a necessary preliminary to the giving of a sign is the taking of a step. The notable exception to this is the sign of R. given during prayers, when a step is not necessary. Some have even claimed that this is not strictly a sign at all, but an *attitude* of R.; it is certainly the case that it is not the sign of any degree. Otherwise, the only exceptions to the general rule are in the Lectures of the three degrees (see Chapter 18), and in the Traditional History of the third degree when the first two signs are demonstrated in the course of the narrative.

In Emulation working, all the signs of the three degrees are given with the hand open throughout. The practice, commonly met with, of closing the fist as the sign is discharged is firmly discouraged as being slovenly, though to many it may appear stylish. Signs are also given silently, except when greeting the newly installed Master during the ceremony of Installation. In fact, the general rule is that all signs should be given quietly and smartly, but without any undue ostentation.

The correct method of giving all the signs is fully detailed in the text and rubric of the Emulation Ritual, but it may be helpful to reinforce the following points. First, in Emulation working the sign of the first degree does not start by placing the hand straight out in front of the body; the hand is brought immediately to the position in which the sign is held. Secondly, the sign of R. differs from the sign of F. in that the thumb lies parallel to, or even concealed by, the fingers, and is discharged by being dropped rather than cut. (It is sometimes debated whether it is the sign of F. or the sign of R. that should be given at the end of the closing, to accompany the words, "F., F., F.". It should be neither: the Lodge is by then closed and therefore any sign is inappropriate; the Brethren merely make a threefold gesture with the r.h. on the l.b..) Thirdly, the first sign of a Master Mason is given in two distinct movements, the first of which is to the front and *not* to the side, still less to the rear: the d. and a.s. is assumed to be directly in front. Fourthly, the p . . . l sign of a Master Mason is given in different ways according to whether it is to be held or to be immediately discharged. In the former case the hand is brought initially to the centre where it is held (in Emulation working the sign is not first given to the point of recovery and then held); when the sign is to be discharged the hand is then carried first to the opposite side. If the sign is to be immediately discharged, for example in opening the Lodge in the third degree or when the Master Masons pass round the Lodge and salute the newly installed Master, the hand is brought immediately direct to the opposite side, without even a momentary pause at the centre. In every case the person giving the sign recovers at the end, except at the moment of opening in the third degree, when recovery is unnecessary, since it has already taken place a minute or two earlier. Finally, when the G. or R. sign is given audibly as a greeting in the Installation ceremony, the first movement is upwards and the sign does *not* begin with a slap of the thighs; when the sign is given silently, the tips of the fingers should touch at the top.

In Emulation working, during an obligation, the Brethren stand to order with the p . . . l sign; the sign of F. is used only in the second degree, not, as in the case of some other workings, whenever an obligation is taken. The sign is discharged as soon as the Candidate has finished repeating the words of the obligation, and before he seals it. In this respect also Emulation differs from many other workings, as well as certain other degrees beyond the Craft. Whilst, however, there may be an argument for holding the sign of F. until the Candidate has sealed, it is difficult to see any obvious reason why a *p . . . l* sign should be held beyond the end of the obligation itself.

The sign of the degree is always given when entering or retiring from the Lodge, except during the ceremony of Installation when Entered Apprentices, Fellow Crafts and Master Masons retire and later re-enter together. A Brother entering the Lodge for the first time during a meeting gives the signs of every degree in which the Lodge has been opened; if he wishes to extend his apologies for his late arrival (which is not the practice in Emulation Lodge of Improvement) he does so while holding the sign of the highest degree. A Brother retiring from the Lodge or returning to it, gives only the sign of the degree in which the Lodge is then open. The only exception to this is a Candidate for Passing or Raising, who gives, under the direction of the Deacon, all the signs of the degrees up to and including the one in which the Lodge is then open.

When the Brethren stand together as part of the ritual they should do so, taking their cue in this – as in many other instances – from the Master, only after the Junior Warden has knocked, and not as soon as the Master has done so.

In Emulation working, the words "So mote it be" are spoken by the Immediate Past Master (i.e. the Preceptor) alone. In most Private Lodges, however, they are said or sung by all the Brethren present.

In the first degree, when the Candidate is restored to light, the Brethren should be careful to synchronise their handclap with the descent of the Master's gavel. Similarly at a later stage when the Senior Warden invests the Candidate.

Towards the end of the explanation of the second degree Tracing Board the sign of R. is given only *after* the words "denoting G." and *not* as soon as the Brethren stand.

During the ceremony of Installation, when the Master Masons, Fellow Crafts and Entered Apprentices perambulate the Lodge, each pauses briefly before the Master's pedestal and, still facing south, gives the sign by way of salute to the newly installed Master. In Emulation, these signs are not given "in passing", and the Lodge is squared. (I should, however, add that in many other workings the signs are given in passing, and that that is the case under the direction of the Grand Director of Ceremonies or one of his Deputies when a Consecration or Installation is carried out by a senior Grand Officer.)

In Emulation working "toward" is regarded as interchangeable with "towards", "while" with "whilst", and "among" with "amongst", though it is probably fair to say that the members of the precepting Committee have a *preference* for whichever appears in the printed ritual, particularly in the case of "toward" and "towards". The words "on" and "upon" are not, however, so regarded, and the correct word must always be used. The reader may, nonetheless, console himself with the thought that there are only three occurrences of "upon" in the whole Emulation ritual – all in the Master's work – and these are detailed in Chapter 15.

The general layout of the Lodge is unlikely to call for much explanation by me. It should, however, be noted that in Emulation Lodge of Improvement only one Tracing Board is used – that of the degree or Lecture which is to be worked. (When the Installation ceremony is being demonstrated, the Tracing Board will have been removed altogether.) It lies in the centre of the floor of the Lodge and is never covered or turned, so that it is exposed to view from before the Lodge is opened until after the Lodge is closed or called off. The Emulation Tracing Boards are very large indeed and moving them would be impracticable. As the Lodge may only be attended by Master Masons, this causes no difficulty, but it is likely to be otherwise in a regular Lodge and the Junior Deacon will generally be responsible for changing the Boards (which customarily rest against the front of the Junior Warden's pedestal) at the appropriate times.

There is sometimes confusion as to whether a Brother standing in for one of the Officers should wear the collar and jewel of that office. The answer is set out clearly in the booklet "Information for the Guidance of Members of the Craft". If the particular Officer is present, he alone may wear the collar, and a Brother temporarily performing his duties for him does not wear it. But if the Officer is absent, the stand-in should wear it.

Another matter where there is uncertainty among many members of the Craft is in relation to the use of the prefix "Worshipful". In Emulation, the only person addressed as "Worshipful" is the Master; and he should *always* be addressed as "Worshipful Master" – never as just "Master". No one else is so addressed, or even referred to, either by name or by reference to his office. Thus "Worshipful Brother Secretary" is contrary to the practice of Emulation Lodge of Improvement, and it is suggested that as a matter of principle it is wrong, since the prefix "Worshipful", except in the case of the Master, belongs to the *individual* and not to the *office*. In Emulation Lodge of Improvement, the nearest approach to addressing an individual as "Worshipful" is the use of the title "Past Master" when addressing, or referring to, members of the Committee, who are to all intents the Past Masters of Emulation Lodge of Improvement. Thus "Brother Past Master Redman" is the accepted method of referring to me during a meeting of the Lodge.

Whilst it cannot be said that to address or refer to someone as "Worshipful Brother Smith" is wrong, there is no doubt in my mind that it is unnecessary. Even less desirable, in my view, is the uneasy mixture of the formal and the informal, more commonly met with at dinner than in the Lodge, represented by the prefix "Worshipful" with a Brother's first name alone. "Brother Smith" is correct Emulation working – and quite sufficient; "Worshipful Brother Smith" is acceptable, as in some cases is "Brother John"; but "Worshipful Brother John" is neither one thing nor the other and really will not do.

It is sometimes said that no ritual or ceremonial practice in Masonry is actually wrong. Clearly this cannot be true; some things *are* wrong, and an example would be the continued use of the penalties in the course of administering the obligations. But what the proponents of this view mean is that there are wide tolerances as to what is permissible. No Brother should forget this, particularly when visiting a Lodge which uses a different working from that with which he is familiar. We are all prone to assume that the way that we do things in our own Lodge is the only – or at any rate the best – way. But just because a Lodge does something differently, we should not be hasty to condemn it as wrong.

Chapter 4

The Tyler

The Tyler ranks last amongst the Officers of a Lodge. He alone of the Officers need not be a subscribing member of the Lodge (see Rule 104(b) of the Book of Constitutions) and generally he is not, but is elected annually and receives a fee for his services. This is the situation in Emulation Lodge of Improvement.

By Rule 113 of the Book of Constitutions, however, a Lodge may resolve that a subscribing member of the Lodge shall be Tyler without emolument. In such a case he is appointed by the Master, along with the other Officers (apart from the Treasurer, who must always be elected).

The Tyler must be a Master Mason and registered as such in the books of Grand Lodge. (A Tyler is sometimes referred to as a "Serving Brother", but the expression is generally misused in this context. A Serving Brother is one initiated by dispensation under the provisions of Rule 170 of the Book of Constitutions. He enjoys – if that is the right word – a peculiarly hobbled status, without any of the rights of a present or former subscribing member of a Lodge, unless he becomes a joining member of a Lodge – and thereupon ceases to be a Serving Brother.) It is, however, most desirable that he should be a Past Master, and preferably one of some experience, since his duties extend far beyond the ceremonial matters described in the ceremony of Opening the Lodge and explained to him at his investiture. Upon him falls, in particular, the preparation of the Lodge Room before the meeting. If a "professional" Tyler is elected annually by the Lodge, he may be expected to be thoroughly conversant with such matters, and the only guidance which he may require will be in relation to the carrying out of his ceremonial duties in accordance with the specific requirements of Emulation working.

The method of preparing the Candidates for the various degrees is adequately detailed in the printed ritual, as are the knocks to be employed. It is, however, worth reiterating the point that in Emulation working the Tyler never gives a single knock to announce that there is a Brother outside the door who requires admission. In the case of a Brother arriving late, or returning to the Lodge, the knocks of the degree in which the Lodge is then open are given. In the case of a Candidate for Passing or Raising, the knocks are those of the highest degree which the Candidate has already received. In the case of a Candidate for Initiation, three distinct knocks are given, at somewhat longer intervals than those of the first degree, so that it is apparent to those inside the Lodge that it is not just a late arrival.

In Emulation a late arrival is announced to the Inner Guard as "Brother ....." or if there is more than one person to be admitted "Brother ..... and other Brethren". (Note that in Emulation Lodge of Improvement even if there is only one additional Brother, the words "and other Brethren" are, by long custom, still used.) Similarly a Brother returning to the Lodge Room after a temporary absence will be announced as "Brother ..... on his return". The prefix "Worshipful" is not used in either form of announcement, nor does the Tyler add the Brother's rank or words such as "seeks admission" at the end; it goes without saying that that is what the Brother wants.

From time to time an official visitor to a Lodge makes a ceremonial entrance with an escort after the Lodge has been opened; in such a situation the Tyler should not necessarily adhere strictly to the foregoing procedure, but must be guided instead as to the form of the announcement he is to make by the Grand Director of Ceremonies, the Metropolitan, Provincial or District Grand Director of Ceremonies, or whoever is deputising in such a capacity.

At the beginning of the ceremony of Initiation, the Candidate must repeat the words "By the help of G. being free and of good report" after the Tyler, in reply to the Inner Guard's second question, and the Tyler must ensure that he does so; sadly, this rarely happens in a regular Lodge. When the Candidate is ready to return to the Lodge after restoring his personal comfort in each of the three degrees, the correct report by the Tyler is "The Candidate on his return" and the Candidate's name should not be used. It is a great help in a regular Lodge if the Tyler spends a few moments before he gives the report in ensuring that the Candidate is proficient in the step(s) and sign(s) which he will need to give when he re-enters the Lodge.

In the ceremony of Installation, when he is summoned by a double knock to be invested, the Tyler enters the Lodge with his sword held point downwards in his left hand, and his collar draped over his left arm. After saluting, he makes his way direct by the shortest route to the north or south side of the Master's pedestal, according to whether he is a Master Mason or a Past Master, and lays the sword diagonally across the V.S.L., taking care not to disturb the Sq. and Cs.. When the sword is returned to him, he receives it with his right hand and immediately transfers it to his left. After the Master has shaken hands with him, he does not salute, but returns to the north of the S.W.'s pedestal by the shortest route, and there salutes before retiring from the Lodge. (I should add here that many senior Brethren believe it wrong in principle for the Tyler's sword to be laid across the V.S.L.. In a regular Lodge, Brethren should follow their conscience in this matter. I should, however, make the point that as Emulation Lodge of Improvement was already working at the time that the form of the Installation ceremony was settled by the Board of Installed Masters in 1827 there is a strong presumption that Emulation's practice in this matter accords with what was settled at that time.)

At the conclusion of dinner, the Tyler, if present, will normally propose the Tyler's toast. On the two occasions in the year when Emulation Lodge of Improvement dines after a meeting, this toast is given by the Tyler. The correct form of the toast is the words of the Charge at the conclusion of the Third Section of the First Lecture, namely: "All poor and distressed Masons, wherever dispersed over the face of earth and water, wishing them a speedy relief from all their sufferings, and a safe return to their native country, if they desire it."

If I seem to the "professional" Tyler to have dealt at considerable length with his ceremonial duties it is partly because such Brethren generally act as Tyler for numerous different Lodges, which between them use a variety of different workings. Under such conditions it is all too easy for "cross-fertilisation" to occur, more often by accident than by any deliberate design on the part of the Tyler. If, on the other hand, a Lodge has availed itself of the provisions of Rule 113, and the Master has appointed a relatively junior Brother to the office, the latter will certainly be at least as much in need of instruction as those of his Brethren a few steps ahead of him "on the ladder". It is also to be hoped that even more senior Brethren will find the guidance given helpful.

Chapter 5

The Inner Guard

In the ordinary course this is the first office which the young Mason holds in which he has ritual duties to perform. It is not an unduly demanding office, but it provides an early opportunity for a Brother to impress his seniors one way or the other. No one can easily overlook the way the Inner Guard conducts himself, and if he is competent in carrying out his duties, the impression he can make is out of all proportion to the amount of effort involved in learning them.

The first, and fundamental, point which every Inner Guard should understand is that *he alone* has charge of the door of the Lodge, and should allow no other Brother, however senior (or impatient), to open or close it. This being so, he should be alert to ensure that when anyone wishes to leave the Lodge he himself precedes that Brother to the door. When the Inner Guard opens the door, he should at all times retain a firm hold on it, (indeed, it is best if he places his foot behind it as well so as to make it difficult for anyone outside to gain entry until he is ready to admit him); when he closes the door, he should always ensure that it is locked as well. These observations apply with no less force at the beginning and end of every meeting than during the course of it. Thus when all the Brethren have entered the Lodge Room and the meeting is about to begin it is the Inner Guard's duty to close and lock the door; similarly after the Lodge is finally closed, the Inner Guard must ensure that he reaches the door in time to unlock and open it so that the Master and Brethren can pass through.

Secondly, the Inner Guard should perform his duties efficiently, but without undue ostentation. In particular, he should be thoroughly familiar with the general remarks contained in Chapter 3. In Emulation working, the Inner Guard occupies the seat on the left of the Senior Warden. The position from which he makes all reports is immediately in front of his chair (with the backs of his knees almost touching the front of the chair), and standing square with his body facing East; he does not advance to the edge of the carpet. When he addresses the Junior Warden he does not turn his body, but after having taken a step and given a sign (if appropriate) he turns only his head.

In opening the Lodge, in each degree, when asked to see that the Lodge is properly tyled, the Inner Guard goes to the door, does not open it, and gives the knocks of the degree in which the Lodge is then open, or in the case of opening in the first degree, the first degree knocks. Once he has given the knocks himself, there is no need for him to wait at the door until they are returned by the Tyler, but he returns at once to his place immediately in front of his chair; the Tyler's knocks will be clearly audible throughout the Lodge. As soon as they have been given, the Inner Guard reports to the Junior Warden. In the first degree opening, he does not take a step or give any sign, and addresses that Brother by name; in the other degrees, he first takes the step and gives the sign of the degree in which the Lodge is then open and addresses him as "Brother Junior Warden". In each case the report in opening is "the Lodge is properly tyled" (whereas in the closing it is "the Lodge is close tyled"). It is unfortunately common among Inner Guards, no doubt anxious to deliver the ritual with *meaning*, to emphasise the word "is". This practice is very firmly discouraged in Emulation Lodge of Improvement. The emphasis is quite unnecessary, and if it conveys any special meaning, it is the suggestion that the Tyler cannot necessarily be relied on to do his job properly, or, worse, that the Junior Warden is displaying an excess of caution in asking his question.

When the Lodge is declared open, the Inner Guard should ensure that he arrives at the door in time to maintain the same interval between the knocks as that set by the Senior and Junior Wardens, and when he gives the knocks, he should duplicate the rhythm of the Master and Wardens; indeed, to maintain the same interval he may, in a large room, need to leave his place before the Junior Warden has given his knocks. Once again there is no need for him to wait at the door for the Tyler to return the knocks. When, however, there is a Candidate for Passing or Raising waiting outside the door, the Master and Wardens will give "silent" knocks – audible only within the Lodge – and the Inner Guard does not go to the door, but merely stands in his place and gives the knocks with his open right hand on the cuff of his left sleeve (ensuring that the rhythm of, and between, the knocks is maintained). On returning to his place at the conclusion of the third degree opening, the Inner Guard must not forget to take a step in readiness for the G. or R. sign.

When the Lodge is resumed from one degree to another, the same procedure is followed as at the end of the opening, the knocks given being those of the degree into which the Lodge is being resumed, and being given on the door or "silently" depending on whether or not there is a Candidate outside.

In closing, the procedure is almost identical to that in the opening, save that the report to the Junior Warden is slightly different, and there can, of course, be no question of the knocks being given silently. It should not need saying that the correct knocks, at both beginning and end of each closing, are those of the degree in which the Lodge is being closed.

In Emulation working a late arrival is announced by the Tyler giving the knocks of the degree in which the Lodge is then open. The Inner Guard should bear in mind that the Tyler may have only a rough idea of what is going on in the Lodge, and that the moment when the knocks are given on the door may not be the most convenient time for the report to be taken. If he is in any doubt as to whether or not the time is right, he should catch the eye of the Junior Warden, to whom he will be announcing the report, and allow himself to be guided by that Officer. Having assured himself that the report may be taken, he stands in his place, gives the sign (not forgetting to take a step first) and announces "Brother Junior Warden, there is a report". He holds the sign until the Junior Warden knocks once, then discharges it and goes to the door, which he unlocks and opens. He says nothing. The Tyler should report the late arrival to the Inner Guard as "Brother ....." or if there be more than one person to be admitted "Brother ..... and other Brethren". Similarly a Brother returning to the Lodge Room after a temporary absence will be announced as "Brother ..... on his return". The prefix "Worshipful" is not used in either form of announcement, nor should the Tyler add the Brother's rank or words such as "seeks admission" at the end. The Inner Guard, still saying nothing closes and locks the door, returns to his place, and reports to the Master with step and sign "Worshipful Master, Brother ....." (or other words in accordance with the formula just given). Even if the Tyler has chosen to add extraneous words, the Inner Guard should *not* do so, but should adhere strictly to the correct formula. It does, of course, happen from time to time that an official visitor to a Lodge makes a ceremonial entrance, accompanied by an escort, after the Lodge has been opened; in such a situation the Inner Guard, like the Tyler, should not necessarily adhere strictly to the foregoing, but must be guided as to the form of the announcement he is to make by the Grand Director of Ceremonies, the Metropolitan, Provincial or District Grand Director of Ceremonies, or whoever is deputising in such a capacity.

In the ceremony of Initiation (and also of Passing and Raising), the Inner Guard must not forget that, having reported to the Junior Warden, he must hold the step and sign until he is told to see who wants admission. At the door of the Lodge, he should conduct his questioning of the Tyler sufficiently loudly to be heard in all parts of the Lodge. Also he should remember that the Candidate has to repeat the Tyler's answer to the second question, and should therefore not be too quick to come in with his own response; indeed, he should not proceed until he has heard the words – which are analogous to a password – from the Candidate's own lips. As he will shortly be asked by the Master to vouch that the Candidate is properly prepared, he should check that he is. Having closed and locked the door, he reports to the Master, remembering that on this occasion, and on this occasion only, the Candidate's name is prefixed by "Mister" and not "Brother". He holds the sign during the following colloquy with the Master until after the words "in due form", when he discharges it. In Emulation Lodge of Improvement the p....d is placed in readiness on the Senior Warden's pedestal, and not as in many Lodges on a ledge just within the door. Accordingly, the Inner Guard must not forget to take it with him to the door. Ideally, he should not move until the Senior Deacon has placed the kneeling stool and the Deacons are themselves ready to move off to the door; he then turns, takes up a position in front of the Deacons and leads the way. This small procession, if properly managed, can be decidedly impressive. In any event, the Inner Guard must not open the door until the Deacons are ready to receive the Candidate. After applying the p....d and receiving an answer to his question, he raises the p....d above his head and then stands aside, still retaining his hold on the door, so that the Junior Deacon may take the Candidate by the hand. Having closed and locked the door he returns behind the Deacons and Candidate to his place and sits, but he must not forget to bring the p....d with him and replace it on the Senior Warden's pedestal. This is particularly liable to be forgotten if the Lodge is one in which the p....d normally reposes on a ledge inside the door.

His duties are then over until the Candidate comes to retire to restore his comfort. At this point in the ceremony, he should rise as the Candidate salutes, turn and take up his position as, or very slightly after, the Junior Deacon wheels the Candidate round, and after a slight pause lead the way to the door. This too, if managed properly, can look very stylish. After closing and locking the door, he returns to his place and sits until such time as the Tyler gives the report. The only observation which needs to be made in relation to reporting the Candidate's return is that even if the Tyler does not use the correct formula for his announcement, the Inner Guard should do so. As soon as he has been told by the Master to admit the Candidate, the Inner Guard discharges the sign, but once again he should not turn and move off to the door until the Junior Deacon has almost drawn level with him. If he observes this point, he will not need to wait at the door for the Junior Deacon to arrive before he opens it to admit the Candidate.

When the Candidate comes to be passed to the second degree, the procedure to be adopted when he leaves the Lodge after being entrusted with the p.g. and p.w. is exactly the same as when he retired to restore his comfort in the previous degree. When the Lodge is opened or resumed in the second degree the Inner Guard should not forget the procedure for "silent" knocks. Nor must he forget – as some do – that, although the Tyler announces the presence of the Candidate by the first degree knocks, the Lodge is now open in the second degree and therefore he must give the *second* degree sign when announcing the report to the Junior Warden.

At this point the procedure follows closely that in the first degree. The Inner Guard retains his hold on the door during the colloquy with the Tyler, which should again be loud enough to be heard in all parts of the Lodge, and although he will not on this occasion be asked for confirmation by the Master, the Inner Guard should again check that the Candidate has been properly prepared. (This is even more important in the third degree when the Lodge will be in darkness and any error on the part of the Tyler may easily pass unnoticed.) When the Candidate is admitted, a point of difference is that the Inner Guard asks no question when he applies the Sq., and if the latter is kept on a ledge by the door, it need not be taken afterwards to the Senior Warden's pedestal (unless there should be no second Sq. at the Master's pedestal, in which case it will be required for use during the Obligation). The procedure for the retirement and readmission of the Candidate is similar to that in the first degree, though, as the signs of both degrees are given by the Candidate on retiring, the Inner Guard should wait a moment or two longer before rising from his seat and turning, so as to time the latter movement with the arrival of the Senior Deacon and Candidate.

In Emulation Lodge of Improvement it is the practice for all the Brethren to stand when the explanation of the Tracing Board is given, and, with the exception of the Wardens, Inner Guard and the Past Master who will gavel near the end, to gather round the Tracing Board. The Inner Guard should therefore not forget to stand fast in his place at this point.

When the Candidate comes to be raised to the third degree, a procedure similar to that in the second is adopted, with the following important differences. First, the Inner Guard should not announce the report until the Deacons have finished laying out the s...t and have returned to their places. Secondly, when he has taken the Cs. and led the Deacons to the door, he must not open it immediately, but must wait until the lights have been lowered, and until any Brother who has been engaged in that operation has resumed his seat. (Indeed, depending on the practice of the individual Lodge, it may be his responsibility to turn off the electric lights.) Only then should he open the door. In this degree, both points of the opened Cs. should be applied simultaneously. Finally, after the prayer, his is the responsibility for replacing the kneeling stool, as the Junior Deacon is engaged in the perambulation.

In the ceremony of Installation, if the Inner Guard is a Master Mason he must be replaced by an Installed Master at some stage before the start of the Inner Working. In Emulation Lodge of Improvement, this may be done either before the Lodge is resumed in the second degree prior to the start of the ceremony, or at the point when the Master Masons retire, in the latter case an Installed Master being asked to take charge of the door at the appropriate moment; if the Inner Guard is already an Installed Master no substitution is made. In a regular Lodge it will generally be convenient to place an Installed Master in the Inner Guard's seat when the Wardens are replaced after the Entered Apprentices have retired. The duties of the Inner Guard during this ceremony are straightforward, and the only point which needs to be noted is that when he is asked by the Installing Master to admit Master Masons, Fellow Crafts or Entered Apprentices, the Inner Guard resumes his seat immediately on his return from the door, without making any announcement. If there are, for example, no Fellow Crafts, he should not, as happens frequently, make some such report as "Brother Installing Master, all Fellow Crafts are admitted."

The first duty of the newly appointed and invested Inner Guard is to admit the Tyler for investiture. When the Master gives a double knock to summon the Tyler, the Inner Guard rises, and proceeds immediately to the door. He admits the Tyler, closes and locks the door, returns to his place and sits. In Emulation working he does not himself leave the Lodge under the pretence of ensuring that the Lodge remains tyled. When the Tyler salutes before leaving the Lodge, the Inner Guard rises, and leads the way to the door, rather as he does when a Candidate retires to restore his comfort in any of the three degrees.

Chapter 6

The Deacons

It is convenient to deal with certain matters which affect both Deacons, as a preliminary to a description of their individual duties, in order to avoid a certain amount of repetition.

The Deacons' duties fall into two categories – the ritual and the procedural. Ironically, it is only the latter which are mentioned at the opening of the Lodge, but the former, which are drawn to the attention of each of the Deacons on his investiture, are much the more important.

In Emulation Lodge of Improvement the Senior Deacon sits in his old position, on the immediate right of the Master, directly facing the Inner Guard. In most regular Lodges, however, the Senior Deacon sits at the extreme eastern end of the front row of seats on the north side of the Lodge. The Junior Deacon occupies the seat immediately to the right of the Senior Warden in the West.

Each Deacon carries a wand as his badge of office, but only during the performance of his ritual duties in the ceremonies of Initiation, Passing and Raising. When he carries it, he should always do so with dignity. While he is on the move, the butt of the wand should be a few inches above the floor, and when he is at rest the butt should rest on the floor of the Lodge. On no account should a Deacon lean upon his wand for support; nor should he carry it other than in his right hand – and in an upright position – except where the ritual specifically requires him to do so.

There is no single correct method of holding the wand; some Deacons hold it in the lightly clenched fist with the forearm parallel to the ground; but the better method is for the Deacon to hold it lightly between the thumb and forefinger, using the remaining fingers of the right hand to steady it, at the point where the hand naturally grasps it if the elbow is very slightly bent and the butt of the wand is resting on the ground. If the wand is supported in this manner, then by bending the elbow so that his forearm is at an angle of forty-five degrees to the horizontal the Deacon can lift his wand to the optimum position for carrying it while he is on the move.

During the ceremony of Initiation the Junior Deacon, and during the ceremony of Passing the Senior Deacon, has charge of the Candidate throughout except at the Master's pedestal when his authority is subordinated to that of his superior. During the ceremony of Raising, the Candidate is in the charge of the Senior Deacon except at the Master's pedestal, and when the Master and Wardens have charge of him following the Exhortation; at some parts of the ceremony he is additionally in the charge of the Junior Deacon. For convenience, the Deacon who primarily has charge of the Candidate is referred to in what follows as the "acting Deacon" and his colleague as the "non-acting Deacon".

In general the acting Deacon takes hold of the Candidate only when he leads him from one part of the Lodge to another. However, it is essential that during the ceremony of Initiation the Junior Deacon should never relinquish his hold on the Candidate's hand while the latter is in darkness, except when he is kneeling or his hand is held by another Officer. As the Notes on Ritual and Procedure in the front of the Emulation Ritual point out, the manner of holding the Candidate is a matter of common sense, and not of ritual. The Deacon should adopt whatever method gives him the greatest degree of control, having regard to the relative heights of himself and the Candidate. It is, however, almost invariably the case that the Deacon will find it easier to manage the Candidate if his left arm is behind the Candidate's right arm, than if it is in front.

The Deacons should be careful to distinguish between those directions and prompts to the Candidate which are printed in black in the Emulation Ritual and those which are merely contained within the rubric. The former are always given aloud, so that they can be heard by all in the Lodge; the latter should only be given in a whisper or a low voice as they do not form a part of the ritual wording.

All instructions in the course of a perambulation, except for directions to the Candidate to salute or advance to one of the principal Officers, are given in a whisper or a low voice. During perambulations, and only during perambulations, the Lodge is squared. On all other occasions the acting Deacon leads the Candidate by the shortest route (i.e. in a straight line). When squaring is to be carried out, the Deacon and Candidate halt, turn right, make a momentary pause, and then step off together with the left foot. In the first and second degrees, the Candidate is the pivot; that is to say, the acting Deacon wheels backwards, while the Candidate turns on his own ground. In the third degree, however, the Senior Deacon must be the pivot so as to allow the Junior Deacon, who is close behind the Candidate, room to square the Lodge before all three step off again together.

Certain features of the Deacons' work are common to the ceremonies of all three degrees; others to those of the first and second degrees only.

After the Master has ordered the admission of the Candidate and called on the Deacons, the acting Deacon makes his way with his wand to the north of the Senior Warden's pedestal, where he waits until the non-acting Deacon has placed the kneeling stool (preferably by drawing it along the floor, whilst keeping his wand *upright*) and has taken up a position on his right; the non-acting Deacon should be careful, if the stool is slightly angled, rather than flat, to check that it is angled in the correct direction. The Deacons should always endeavour to ensure that they set off to the door simultaneously with the Inner Guard; it has already been noted in the chapter on the Inner Guard that, if properly carried out, this small procession can be very impressive. It should be remembered that on the way to the door, the acting Deacon is always on the left in each of the three degrees, so that when the procession reaches the door and the Deacons turn about he will be to the right of the Candidate. When the Inner Guard steps aside after elevating the p.....d, Sq. or Cs., the acting Deacon takes the Candidate firmly by the right hand, whispers instructions, leads him to the kneeling stool and halts.

When the Master gavels for the prayer, each Deacon transfers his wand to his left hand to cross it above the Candidate's head, and gives the sign of R. with his right. It is quite immaterial, in Emulation working, whether the acting Deacon's wand is crossed in front of the non-acting Deacon's, or *vice versa*.

Just as it is the duty of the non-acting Deacon to place the kneeling stool before going to the door, so it is his duty to draw it aside after the Candidate has risen following the prayer. He also replaces it in front of the Senior Warden's pedestal, except in the third degree when the Junior Deacon is engaged in the perambulation and the duty falls instead to the Inner Guard.

After the recital of the prayer, the Candidate is conducted round the Lodge. There is one perambulation in each degree which the Candidate has already received, and one perambulation, preceded by an announcement from the Master, for the degree to which he is about to be admitted. In Emulation working, the Deacon does not take a step and give the sign with the Candidate.

In Emulation Lodge of Improvement (and most regular Lodges) the layout of the Lodge Room is such that to lead the Candidate to the side of the Junior Warden's pedestal, the acting Deacon has to carry out a "sideways shuffle" to the left, reversing the procedure in order to regain the floor of the Lodge after the examination. Where, however, space permits, there can be no objection (except in the third degree when the Junior Deacon is following behind) to this manoeuvre being carried out by a "double wheeling" movement; that is, by the Deacon wheeling backwards using the Candidate as a pivot, as during squaring, and then stepping off, describing a wider wheel, to bring the Candidate back on to the floor of the Lodge.

When at the side of the Wardens' pedestals the acting Deacon and Candidate should stand square (i.e. facing west at the Junior Warden's, and north at the Senior Warden's pedestal) and the Deacon should turn only his head to address the Warden.

When the Lodge is to be squared immediately before conducting the Candidate to the south side of the Senior Warden's pedestal, it is important that the acting Deacon continues in a westerly direction, stepping off the carpet if necessary, until he and the Candidate are level with (i.e. due south of) the side of the pedestal. The Lodge is then squared in the normal fashion. It should be noted in this connection that even if the Lodge Room is very narrow, at least one step must be taken by the Deacon and Candidate after the turn, in order to complete the action of squaring.

When the Candidate has to be conducted from the south to the north side of the Senior Warden's pedestal, this may be carried out either by a "sideways shuffle" on to the floor of the Lodge, followed by a wheeling movement, or by the Deacon wheeling the Candidate backwards so that he faces east, and then describing a semi-circular wheel from one side of the pedestal to the other. Whichever method is adopted, this particular manoeuvre is always followed by the acting Deacon placing the Candidate's hand in that of the Senior Warden. After doing so, he takes up a position on the Candidate's left, and ensures that the latter is facing east. This is particularly important when the Candidate for initiation is still in darkness.

The method of advancing from west to east in each degree before the Obligation is detailed under the duties of the individual Deacons. When the Candidate is asked if he is willing to take the Obligation, the acting Deacon must *not* prompt him to answer in the affirmative; if the Candidate hesitates or seems at a loss the Deacon should whisper "Answer", but the choice must be the Candidate's own. During the Obligation the Deacons hold their wands in their left hands, crossed over the Candidate's head, as at the prayer. Again it is immaterial which wand is in front of the other. On this occasion, however, each takes a step and gives the sign with his right hand (except for the Junior Deacon in the second degree). They lower their wands when the sign is discharged, that is, immediately after the Candidate has repeated the final words of the Obligation and *before* he seals it on the V.S.L..

During the entrustment which follows in the first and second degrees, the Candidate is still in the charge of the Master. The acting Deacon should therefore intervene only if it is absolutely necessary. (The Deacon does not take a step or give the sign with the Candidate.) When he comes to dictate to the Candidate the answers he is to give in the colloquy with the Master, it is essential that he is exceedingly quick off the mark in giving the prompt for the answer to the third question, in order to ensure that the Candidate does not speak the word.

When, during the perambulation which follows (in the course of which the Lodge is squared), the Deacon addresses the Wardens with step and sign, he does not transfer his wand to the left hand. The correct method is for him to rest the butt of the wand on the floor and the top of it in the crook of his right shoulder. Depending on the nature of the floor covering at the particular spot, he may find it necessary to lodge the butt of the wand against the foot of the pedestal or the candlestick to prevent it from slipping. Just as in the earlier perambulation, the Deacon does not take the step or give the sign with the Candidate. After he has placed the Candidate's hand in that of the Warden for the communication of the Tn., he adjusts the Candidate's thumb *from above*. He must always ensure that the phrases in which he dictates the responses to the Candidate are of a sensible length, which the Candidate will have no difficulty in repeating. It is of particular importance that at the Senior Warden's pedestal the Deacon whispers to the Candidate to take the step only, and he must be ready, if necessary, to lay a gentle restraining hand on the Candidate's arm. It is also important that when the Candidate explains to what the (p . . . l) sign alludes, the Deacon dictates the answer in the correct tense – "would rather *have had* his ...." – and that he ensures that the Candidate synchronises his action with the words.

When the Candidate is invested with the badge of the degree, the acting Deacon may assist the Senior Warden, if necessary, during the act of clothing, but he must stand facing east when the Senior Warden addresses the Candidate. As the Senior Warden sits, he takes up a position between the Warden and the Candidate, both of them facing east; it is not necessary to advance to the edge of the carpet.

When the acting Deacon conducts the Candidate to the Master's pedestal for the explanation of the W.Ts. in the first or second degree, this also should be done in a wide wheeling movement.

When the Candidate retires to restore his comfort in either of the first two degrees, the acting Deacon wheels him forwards (anti-clockwise) at the Master's pedestal, leads him direct to the north of the Senior Warden's pedestal, wheels backwards (clockwise), and directs him to salute. After the Candidate has done so, he then wheels with him forwards again and leads him to the door of the Lodge, endeavouring to synchronise the latter movement with the Inner Guard. This procedure illustrates two basic principles to be observed by both Deacons: first, that when the Candidate has to execute an about-turn from east to west, or *vice versa*, the acting Deacon should always keep himself between the Candidate and the Master's pedestal; and secondly that, as has already been mentioned, except during a perambulation, the Lodge is not squared, but the shortest route is taken.

During the questions before Passing and Raising it is the duty of the acting Deacon to prompt the Candidate in his answers if it should prove necessary; he must therefore ensure that he is familiar with the answers himself. Once the Candidate has answered the questions, the Deacon conducts him direct to the north of the Master's pedestal for entrustment. After the Candidate has been entrusted with the p.g. and p.w. by the Master, the acting Deacon leads him direct to the north of the Senior Warden's pedestal, wheels him backwards, directs him to salute, then, after he has done so, wheels him forwards and leads him, in step with the Inner Guard, to the door of the Lodge.

In the ceremony of Raising, there are several additional features in the procedure. As soon as the Lodge has been opened or resumed in the third degree, the Deacons lay out the s...t. In Emulation working the s...t is always laid fully open, and it is the responsibility of the Senior Deacon to select the correct distance from the front of the Master's pedestal. The method of spreading the s...t is a matter of common sense, but it is astonishing how frequently it is done in an untidy or unmethodical fashion. The best method of carrying out the procedure is as follows.

The Junior Deacon collects the s...t – usually from the Senior or Junior Warden's pedestal, though in Emulation Lodge of Improvement it is placed for convenience beneath the Tracing Board – and brings it to the Senior Deacon, who has meanwhile selected the spot for the eastern side of the s...t. The s...t will normally have been folded in three lengthways, parallel to the centre-line of the g...e, and then folded or rolled in the other direction. The s...t should, if possible, be unfolded or unrolled only in one direction, and not fully opened, before being laid (correctly orientated, and still folded in three) on the floor. Once the central portion of the s...t is in position, the sides can be spread. Each Deacon places a foot as an anchor at the centre point of his end (if one Deacon uses his right foot, the other must use his left), then taking the corner of the s...t in his opposite hand carries that hand and the corresponding foot away from the centre of the s...t, thus spreading one side. He then brings that foot back to the centre, places it on the s...t to keep it anchored, and repeats the process with the other hand and foot, thus spreading the other side. The correct and co-ordinated use of this method will ensure that the s...t is laid swiftly and smoothly, and without any significant creases. It also looks extremely stylish. A broadly similar procedure in reverse is followed to refold the s...t, though the foot is placed a third of the way along the end of the s...t in order to make each fold and it may be necessary to change hands in the act of folding.

Once the Master has raised the Candidate after the Obligation in the third degree and resumed his seat, the Deacons back the Candidate between them to the foot of the g...e. This means that all three will normally be standing on the s...t, though the Candidate must not be on the g...e itself. The Deacons do not hold the Candidate's hands. When the Wardens are summoned by the Master at the end of the Exhortation, the Deacons stand fast until each is tapped on his inside shoulder by the appropriate Warden. Each then takes one pace sideways to enable the Warden to stand between him and the Candidate. The line of five thus formed is held for a moment, and then the Deacons turn outwards and return behind the Wardens and Candidate to their places, taking care not to step on the g...e.

In the ceremony of Installation the Deacons have no duties to perform. There is, however, one point which deserves attention. When each Deacon is invested, he is entrusted with his wand. This he transfers momentarily to his left hand in order to shake hands with the Master. That done, he immediately transfers it back to his right hand, so that when he is conducted to his seat by the Installing Master (or Director of Ceremonies) the latter takes him by the right wrist or forearm. The wand should *not* be carried in the left hand at this point.

I have already stated that in Emulation Lodge of Improvement the Deacons carry their wands only when performing their ritual duties in the ceremonies of the three degrees. Their procedural duties generally involve fetching and carrying, and in the execution of these a wand is an embarrassment.

The most important of these duties is the conducting of ballots. In Emulation Lodge of Improvement, the Junior Deacon distributes the tokens, starting with the Immediate Past Master, and passing in a clockwise direction round the Lodge so that he finishes with the Master. He should hand a token to each member of the Lodge, and should on no account offer the bag or box. He then returns to his place and sits.

The Senior Deacon, meanwhile, takes the ballot box to the south side of the Master's pedestal, where he stands square, facing north, while the ballot box is checked. He then collects the tokens starting with the Immediate Past Master, and finishing with the Master, whose token he collects at the north side of his pedestal. He then proceeds to the south side, where he again stands square, facing north, until the result of the ballot has been declared. He then replaces the ballot box on the Secretary's table, returns to his place and sits.

In Emulation Lodge of Improvement there is no occasion for a "paper" ballot, but the above method will do equally well for such a purpose. Some Masons hold that the Master, as the most important person in the Lodge, should be the first to receive a token or paper, and the first to cast his vote. The Emulation practice is, however, that given above, and may easily be justified by an appeal to the very same principle, on the basis that the progression is an upward one, by way of the Junior Warden, then the Senior, through the Grand Officers to the Master.

In Emulation Lodge of Improvement, it is also part of the Deacons' duties to collect the dues at each meeting. The Senior Deacon starts with the Immediate Past Master and finishes with the Senior Warden. The Junior Deacon starts with the Inner Guard and finishes with the Master. Each takes his bag straight to the Secretary's table as soon as he has finished his collection.

Chapter 7

The Junior Deacon

This office is generally the second involving ritual duties to which a Brother is appointed during his progress towards the Chair. It is, however, one of the most important and responsible in all Masonry. It is the Junior Deacon who, in the ceremony of Initiation, first has significant contact with the Candidate on his admission into the Lodge, and he, almost as much as the Master, can make or mar that ceremony. Until his restoration to light the Candidate is heavily dependent on the Junior Deacon, and it is therefore essential that the latter is not only thoroughly conversant with his duties, but is also able to carry them out with *confidence*. If, as sometimes happens, the Junior Deacon is almost as nervous as the Candidate, peril lurks at every turn.

The Junior Deacon should ensure that he is thoroughly familiar with the general matters dealt with in Chapter 3 and the last chapter, as well as the specific duties which are described below.

In Emulation Lodge of Improvement the Junior Deacon has no duties to perform during the ceremonies of opening and closing the Lodge in the three degrees. The Tracing Boards are too large to be changed while the Lodge is at labour, and it is the practice to display only the Tracing Board of the degree which is being demonstrated, or which relates to the Lecture which is being worked. Its position is on the floor in the centre of the Lodge, and it remains there from the time before the Lodge is opened until it is called off or closed. When the ceremony of Installation is demonstrated, no Tracing Board is displayed. In the majority of regular Lodges which use Emulation working the Tracing Boards rest against the Junior Warden's pedestal, and it is one of the duties of the Junior Deacon to change the Tracing Board when the Lodge is opened, closed or resumed. It is probably best that the Junior Deacon should not move from his place to do this until the Junior Warden has given the knocks of the degree. He does not need to carry his wand to do so, though as this manoeuvre is not one that is carried out in Emulation Lodge of Improvement, it cannot be said that he is wrong if he does carry it. On returning to his place at the conclusion of the third degree opening, the Junior Deacon must not forget to take a step in readiness for the G. or R. sign.

During the ceremony of Initiation the Junior Deacon has charge of the Candidate. I have already stressed the need for the Junior Deacon to be confident in the carrying out of his duties in this ceremony. Equally important, however, is that the Junior Deacon should not relinquish his hold on the hand of the Candidate while the latter is in darkness, except while he is kneeling or his hand is held by another Officer.

After the Master has ordered the Candidate's admission and called on the Deacons, the Junior Deacon makes his way with his wand to the north of the Senior Warden's pedestal, and, accompanied by the Senior Deacon, thence to the door in the manner described in the preceding chapter. When the Inner Guard steps aside after elevating the p....d, the Junior Deacon takes the Candidate firmly – this is particularly important in this degree – by the right hand, whispers instructions, leads him to the kneeling stool, and halts. The prompt for the answer to the Master's question is given aloud. When the Candidate is directed to kneel, the Junior Deacon whispers such instructions as are necessary, and once the Candidate has complied, relinquishes his hold on his hand. When the Master gavels, he transfers his wand to his left hand to cross it above the Candidate's head, and gives the sign of R. with his right. After the further examination by the Master, during which he prompts the Candidate aloud, he assists him to rise, but not before the Master has delivered the words "..... no danger can ensue"; he then waits until the Master has made his announcement.

All instructions to the Candidate in the course of the succeeding perambulation are given in a whisper. The method of conducting the Candidate, and of squaring the Lodge, has been described in the previous chapter. The first halt is made at the east side of the Junior Warden's pedestal, and the three blows are to be given firmly, but not so hard as to cause discomfort to any of the parties involved. At the conclusion of the colloquy, the Deacon and Candidate regain the floor of the Lodge and proceed to the south side of the Senior Warden's pedestal where the procedure is repeated; the Junior Deacon should pay particular attention to the method of squaring the south-west corner of the Lodge as described in the last chapter. After the colloquy, the Candidate is conducted to the north side of the pedestal for presentation to the Master. After he has placed the Candidate's right hand in the Senior Warden's left, the Junior Deacon must ensure that the Candidate turns to face east before taking up a position to his left, also facing east.

After the Master has replied to the Warden's presentation, the Junior Deacon must be ready to receive the Candidate's hand back from the Senior Warden, and to take up a position on the Candidate's right. In effect the Candidate and Deacon simply change places at this juncture; there is no need at all for the Junior Deacon to lead the Candidate forward to the edge of the carpet. He retains his hold on the Candidate's hand during the questions which follow and gives the prompts for the answers aloud.

On receiving the direction from the Senior Warden, the Deacon leads the Candidate to a point four to five feet in front of the Master's pedestal. If he is prudent, he will have selected and mentally marked the spot before the start of the meeting. He whispers to the Candidate to place his feet together, and then to turn the right foot out at a right angle in the form of a square. The succeeding instructions are given aloud, and the Deacon advances with the Candidate, controlling the length of the steps, though *not* himself taking the steps in the same manner.

When the Master puts his question to the Candidate before the

Obligation, the Deacon must not prompt the actual answer, but if the Candidate hesitates for more than a moment or two, he may whisper "Answer" to him. He must not forget to raise the Candidate's hand at the appropriate moment in what follows. For the Obligation, the Deacon transfers his wand to his left hand to cross it over the Candidate's head, and gives the sign, not forgetting to take a step.

When the Candidate is directed to seal his Obligation, the Deacon should not apply pressure to the back of his head unless the Candidate hesitates, and then only gentle pressure should be used – by way of indication rather than by way of force.

The method of restoring the Candidate to light should not present any difficulty. The Deacon rests the butt of his wand on the ground and the top in the crook of his right shoulder, and unties the bow, while holding the h.....k firmly in place. He catches the Master's eye as soon as he is ready, and synchronises the removal of the h.....k with the descent of the gavel (see Chapter 15).

After the Candidate has been raised and the Master has resumed his seat, the Junior Deacon leads the Candidate to the north side of the Master's pedestal, close to the latter, but not so close that the Candidate will be unable to take a step. The Candidate has now been restored to light and the Junior Deacon therefore does not retain hold of his hand.

During the explanation of the "three great dangers", the Junior Deacon should ensure that he removes the c.t. from the Candidate's n..k as the Master concludes his remarks about the p....d. This procedure is carried out with the left hand, grasping the c.t. at the point of the n...e (which should be well open) and lifting it *forward* over the Candidate's head so as not to catch it on his chin or nose. The n...e should not be undone unless it is absolutely necessary, and in such a case the Junior Deacon should re-thread it before he hands it to the Master.

The procedure during the entrustment, the subsequent perambulation, and the investiture with the badge has been described in the preceding chapter. When the Senior Warden addresses the Candidate immediately after his investiture, however, the Junior Deacon must not forget to strike his own badge (with his right hand) when the other Brethren strike theirs.

When he is directed by the Master to place the Candidate at the north-east part of the Lodge, the Junior Deacon leads the Candidate not to the north-east corner, but to a point a pace or two short of it.

In Emulation Lodge of Improvement, at the "charity test", the Junior Deacon does not use an alms dish, but standing on the mid-line of the Lodge in front of and facing the Candidate, extends his open left hand towards the latter. If the Candidate is slow in replying, he does not wait for an answer, but proceeds immediately with the next question, and in any event drops his hand before asking the remaining questions. In a regular Lodge, if an alms dish is used it should be handed discreetly by the Almoner (or some other conveniently placed Brother) to the Junior Deacon during the preceding address, and the latter should not have to move to collect it himself. If the Junior Deacon has taken up the correct position to direct the questions to the Candidate, then once he has concluded his questioning, he need only make a simple right turn in order to address the Master. When he salutes in the course of so doing, he does not transfer his wand to his left hand, but rests it in the crook of his right shoulder as at the restoration to light. Before the Master replies, he rejoins the Candidate and takes up a position on his right.

The procedure during the rest of the ceremony has already been dealt with in the previous chapter. At the conclusion of the Charge after Initiation, the Junior Deacon leads the Candidate to a seat on the immediate right of the Senior Deacon (see "Information for the Guidance of Members of the Craft") and resumes his seat.

In the ceremony of Passing, the Junior Deacon has charge of the Candidate only during the questioning and subsequent entrustment with the p.g. and p.w.. As the non-acting Deacon, his duties during the remainder of the ceremony are relatively straightforward. He should, however, note the following points.

He is in attendance on the Candidate during the Obligation, and he must time his arrival at the Master's pedestal to coincide with that of the Senior Deacon and Candidate. He should endeavour to perform this manoeuvre unobtrusively and without undue haste. Clearly, the correct timing to achieve this is a matter of experience, and will depend, among other things, on the size of the Lodge Room, but in general if the Junior Deacon leaves his place at the moment when the Senior Deacon, having concluded his demonstration of the steps, leads the Candidate forward to the f..t of the w.s., he will find that he can move smoothly and without haste so as to arrive at the pedestal at the right moment.

While the Master is instructing the Candidate to take up his position for the Obligation, the Senior Deacon passes the Sq. behind the Candidate to the Junior Deacon. The Junior Deacon, synchronising his actions with the Master's words, raises the Candidate's left arm, and supports it in the angle of the Sq., which he holds in his right hand. The Candidate's upper arm should be parallel to the ground and extended straight to the front, his forearm perpendicular, and the thumb of his hand (which has the palm to the right, not to the front) bent back in the form of a sq., parallel to the upper arm. If, as is generally the case, the arms of the Sq. are of unequal length, it should be the longer which runs along the Candidate's forearm, and the shorter along his upper arm. As his right hand is engaged, the Junior Deacon does not give the sign during the Obligation, though he does take a step and cross his wand over the Candidate's head. Before the Candidate seals the Obligation, the Junior Deacon lowers the latter's hand to his side, and returns the Sq. to the Senior Deacon. As soon as the Candidate has been raised after the Obligation, the Junior Deacon turns about, returns to his place by the shortest route and sits.

When the Senior Deacon leads the Candidate to the foot of the Tracing Board on the latter's return to the Lodge, the Junior Deacon leaves his place to take up a position on the Candidate's left. He hands his wand to the Master (or whoever is delivering the

Explanation of the Tracing Board), and receives it back at the end. If, as in Emulation Lodge of Improvement, the Tracing Board is so large that it is necessary for one or other party to move to effect the handover, it is, of course, the Junior Deacon who must do so.

During the ceremony of Raising, the Junior Deacon is in attendance on the Candidate from the time when he is admitted to the Lodge until he is delivered into the charge of the Wardens. He does not, therefore, replace the kneeling stool after drawing it aside following the prayer, but sets off at once on the perambulations, which are conducted in the manner described in the last chapter. He must keep as close as possible behind the Candidate. It should help him to keep both close to the Candidate and in step if he ensures that he steps off simultaneously with the Senior Deacon and Candidate, but takes a very short first step. At the end of the first perambulation, the north-west corner of the Lodge is squared as in the course of the perambulations. At the end of the second peram-bulation, the Junior Deacon passes behind the Senior Deacon and Candidate to take up a position on the left of the latter for the Master's announcement. At the end of the third perambulation, when the Senior Deacon wheels the Candidate to the north side of the Senior Warden's pedestal, the Junior Deacon continues in a straight line for a couple of paces further than the Senior Deacon and the Candidate, before wheeling himself to take up a position on the left of the former.

After the Deacons have been directed by the Senior Warden to instruct the Candidate to advance to the east, the Junior Deacon moves off in formation behind the Senior Deacon and Candidate as before. While the Senior Deacon halts the Candidate and turns him to face south, the Junior Deacon passes behind them to take up a position on the Candidate's left, also facing south. He does not accompany the Candidate when the latter advances by the proper steps, but as in the previous degree times his arrival at the pedestal to coincide with that of the Senior Deacon and Candidate.

The procedure at the Obligation is straightforward, and the remainder of the Junior Deacon's duties in this ceremony have been described in the last chapter.

Chapter 8

The Senior Deacon

This is the third of the "progressive" offices with ritual duties. Those duties are more extensive than those of the Junior Deacon, in that the Senior Deacon has charge of the Candidate in two ceremonies, but they are not more important or more demanding.

The Senior Deacon, like the Junior Deacon, should ensure that he is thoroughly familiar with the general matters dealt with in Chapter 3 and Chapter 6, as well as the specific duties which are described below.

In Emulation Lodge of Improvement the Senior Deacon has no duties to perform during the ceremonies of opening and closing the Lodge in the three degrees.

In the ceremony of Initiation the Senior Deacon has few duties, and they have been largely dealt with in Chapter 6. He should, however, note the following points.

When he has replaced the kneeling stool after the prayer, the Senior Deacon carries the p....d from the Senior Warden's pedestal to the Master's pedestal. He places it directly on to the Master's pedestal and does not hand it to the Master himself.

He should take care to time his arrival at the Master's pedestal before the Obligation so that it coincides with that of the Junior Deacon and the Candidate. At the appropriate point he must not forget to raise the Candidate's left hand so that the Master may position the Cs. in it; similarly, at the end of the Obligation he must be ready to assist in lowering the Candidate's left hand after the Master has removed the Cs. As soon as the Candidate has been raised after the Obligation, the Senior Deacon makes a left turn, returns to his place and sits. After the Obligation, he has no further duties during the ceremony.

During the ceremony of Passing the Senior Deacon has charge of the Candidate from the time that the latter is admitted. It may be helpful to point out that when a prayer is about to be delivered after a Candidate has re-entered the Lodge, he is directed to *advance*; on other occasions he is directed (as on retiring) to *salute* the Worshipful Master. In this degree, and also the third, he must ensure that the Candidate gives the sign of R., adjusting his thumb if necessary, when he kneels for the prayer, and he must also check that he drops it afterwards. The two perambulations follow the pattern described in Chapter 6 and should present no difficulty. The Senior Deacon should, however, be careful that the Candidate, when he halts on the floor of the Lodge level with the Master's or a Warden's pedestal and is directed to salute, does not turn his head or body towards the Officer being saluted, but continues to face to the front. When he is directed by the Senior Warden to instruct the Candidate to advance to the east, he leads him to a point on the north side of the Lodge opposite the imaginary foot of the w.s., turns him to face south and moves to the centre-line of the Lodge.

If there is one procedure in Emulation working which more than any other is consistently carried out incorrectly in Private Lodges, it is the method of advancing from west to east in this degree. The first – and essential – point which the Senior Deacon must grasp is that the imaginary w.s. runs in a semi-circle from a point on the centre-line of the Lodge about two yards short of the Master's pedestal to a point on the centre-line of the Lodge directly in front of the pedestal. It does not, despite the illustration shown on most Tracing Boards (including that used in Emulation Lodge of Improvement), take the form of a quarter circle starting on the north side of the Lodge and ending directly in front of the Master's pedestal, but that is a mistake very commonly made. The second point is that the Candidate must arrive at the pedestal with his feet together in the form of a square, left foot pointing north and right foot pointing east, so that he is able to kneel, without further movement, in the proper attitude. The correct method of performing the manoeuvre is as follows.

Having positioned the Candidate on the north side of the Lodge facing south, the Senior Deacon proceeds, as already mentioned, to the foot of the imaginary w.s., where he briefly addresses the Candidate. He then turns about, and immediately places his feet in the form of a square, left foot pointing south and right foot pointing west. He steps off with the left foot, which he places pointing due south. The second step, with the right foot, is taken in a south-easterly direction; the third, with the left foot, is taken due east; the fourth, with the right foot, north-east; and the fifth step, with the left foot, is taken to a point immediately in front of the pedestal, that foot pointing north, and the right foot being brought in a closing motion heel to heel with the left in the form of a square. Note the following points:

(a)   Each step is taken at forty-five degrees to the preceding one.

(b)   At each step the foot must be raised rather higher than in the ordinary course of walking, to signify the upward direction of the w.s.. This movement should not, however, be exaggerated; a little short of knee-height is quite sufficient.

(c)   The Senior Deacon does *not* give a running commentary on the procedure.

The Senior Deacon, having reached the pedestal, then turns right, and following the line of the w.s. in the reverse direction, but with an ordinary walking motion and without slavishly following the precise position of the individual steps, makes his way back to the Candidate. He takes him by the right hand and leads or draws him to the foot of the w.s., directing him to place his feet in the form of a square. He then releases his hand. In this degree, unlike the former, the Senior Deacon does not tell the Candidate first to place his feet together and then turn the right one out; instead he ensures that he comes *straight into* the starting position. All instructions for this and the succeeding procedure are given in a whisper or low voice. The Senior Deacon does not hold the Candidate's hand when he advances up the w.s., but directs him by standing a little in front of and facing him, and indicating with the butt of his wand the correct position for the next step. When the Candidate arrives at the pedestal, he takes up a position on his right.

Before the Obligation he receives the Sq. from the Immediate Past Master at the appropriate moment and passes it, behind the Candidate, to the Junior Deacon. At the end of the Obligation, he receives it back again and returns it to the Immediate Past Master. At the sealing of the Obligation, the Senior Deacon should not touch the back of the Candidate's head unless it is absolutely necessary.

Once the Candidate has been raised by the Master, the Senior Deacon leads him to the north side of the Master's pedestal, taking care that there is sufficient room for the Candidate to take two steps. The procedure during the entrustment, the subsequent perambulation, and the investiture with the badge is described in Chapter 6.

When directed by the Master to place the Candidate at the south-east part of the Lodge, the Senior Deacon leads him via the north and east, squaring the Lodge. This might appear to be an exception to the general rule that the Lodge is squared only in the course of a perambulation, but in truth, this particular movement should be regarded as the continuation of the perambulation. The Senior Deacon should note that as the Lodge has to be squared at the south-east corner, it is essential that he and the Candidate take at least one step along the south side of the Lodge to complete the process, before he wheels backwards so that he and the Candidate are facing north.

The procedure during the remainder of the ceremony presents little difficulty. Once the Candidate has saluted on his readmission to the Lodge, the Senior Deacon leads him direct to the foot of the Tracing Board for the Explanation. At the conclusion of the Explanation, he must not forget to take the Candidate to a seat in the

Lodge. No particular place is prescribed in Emulation working. Some might argue that just as the Initiate is given a seat in the north-east part of the Lodge, the Candidate who has just been passed should be accommodated in the south-east part. This is not, however, a matter of ritual, and Lodges may follow their own inclination.

During the ceremony of Raising, the Senior Deacon has charge of the Candidate throughout, except when he is under the direction of the Master and his Wardens. The procedure for entrustment with the p.g. and p.w. has been detailed in Chapter 6. As soon as the Lodge has been opened or resumed in the third degree, the Senior Deacon selects the position where the s...t is to be laid. If he takes four good paces diagonally from his place to the mid-line of the Lodge, he should find that the point at which he arrives is the right place for the eastern edge of the s...t (not the eastern edge of the g...e), and he should not move from that point, but should wait for the Junior Deacon to bring the s...t to him. Except to remind the Senior Deacon of the slightly different method of squaring the Lodge required in the perambulations in this degree, and that he will need to leave room for the Junior Deacon to take up a position on the Candidate's left when a halt is made at the end of the second perambulation, the ceremony calls for no comment down to the time when the Senior Warden directs the Deacons to instruct the Candidate to advance to the east.

This is another procedure which is rarely carried out correctly. The Senior Deacon conducts the Candidate, followed by the Junior Deacon, to a point on the north side of the Lodge level with the centre of the s...t. He wheels the Candidate to face south, releases his hand and proceeds to a point half way along the south side of the s...t (without stepping on the latter if he can avoid it), where he briefly addresses the Candidate. He then goes straight to the head of the g...e, and immediately places his feet in the form of a square, left foot pointing east and right foot pointing south. He steps off with the left foot, which he places pointing due north about *a third* of the way along the north edge of the g...e, rapidly bringing up his right foot in the form of a square. The second step, starting with the right foot, is taken to a point *two-thirds* of the way along the south edge of the g...e, rapidly closing with the left foot as before, so that the right foot points south and the left east. The third step, starting with the left foot, is taken to the foot of the g...e, rapidly closing with the right foot, so that the left foot points east and the right south. The procedure is completed by four ordinary paces, starting with the left foot, not forgetting to close the fourth step with the left foot, so as to bring the heels together. Note the following points:

(a) The first three steps are awkward, and it is vital that momentum is maintained by bringing the hind foot up to the leading foot *rapidly*. This comment applies with at least equal force when the Candidate comes to advance a few moments later. If either Senior Deacon or Candidate pauses with his feet straddling the g...e, the manoeuvre is not only rendered extremely difficult, if not impossible, but looks more than faintly ridiculous.

(b) The first two steps present a special difficulty in that the leading foot finishes pointing in a direction diametrically opposite to that from which the hind foot starts. Apart from maintaining the momentum, as already urged, the Deacon will find it easiest if in each case he rests the heel of the leading foot on the finishing point, but with the toes pointing east, and pivots on his heel into the correct position as he closes with the hind foot. In practice, it is a counsel of perfection to expect a Candidate (particularly as the Lodge is in darkness) to orientate his feet correctly after the first and second steps and the Senior Deacon should be content if the Candidate's feet are the correct distance along the g...e.

(c) The third step is frequently rendered more difficult by the Senior Deacon or the Candidate not moving far enough along the g...e at the first and second steps. If the points mentioned at (a) and (b) are observed, both Deacon and Candidate should be able to achieve a greater forward advance on the first two steps.

(d) The Senior Deacon does not deliver a running commentary as he carries out the procedure.

The Senior Deacon returns to the Candidate via the south side of the s...t. He takes him by the right hand and leads or draws him to the head of the g...e, directing him to place his feet in the form of a square. He then releases his hand. In this degree, as in the second, the Deacon does not tell the Candidate first to place his feet together and then turn the right one out; instead he ensures that he comes *straight into* the starting position. All instructions for this and the succeeding procedure are given in a whisper or low voice. The Senior Deacon does not hold the Candidate's hand when he advances along the g...e, but directs him by standing on the south side of the g...e, a little ahead of the Candidate, and indicating with the butt of his wand the correct position for the next step. Similarly, he does not hold the Candidate's hand during the last four steps, but walks beside him to the pedestal, where he takes up a position on his right.

The procedure down to the time when the Wardens take charge of the Candidate has already been dealt with in Chapter 6. When the Master concludes the communication of the secrets, the Senior Deacon goes straight to the right of the Candidate, taking care not to cross the path of the Master as the latter returns to the Chair. He takes him by the right hand and leads him to the north of the Senior Warden's pedestal, where he instructs him to salute the Master, remembering to give him the direction "P...l sign only in the third" in a low voice or a whisper.

On the Candidate's return, the direction "Full signs" is similarly given *sotto voce*. The Senior Deacon then takes the Candidate by the right hand and draws him backwards to the Senior Warden to be presented for investiture. After the Master's address he leads the Candidate to a point about two feet in front of the Master's pedestal.

His only duties during the remainder of the ceremony are to ensure that the Candidate does not take a step before the signs which are demonstrated incidentally in the course of the narrative, but that he does take a step during the full explanation. The Candidate does *not* repeat any words at the latter point. Once the ceremony has been completed, he must not forget to take the Candidate to a seat in the Lodge, though there may be a short delay as the Master may well wish to congratulate him – and perhaps to present him with a ritual and a pair of gloves.

In Emulation Lodge of Improvement, the Minutes are not signed by the Master. In a regular Lodge, however, it is the duty of the Senior Deacon to carry the Minute Book to the Master for signature. He does not carry his wand when doing so. On no account should he rest the Minute Book on the V.S.L. while the Master signs.

Chapter 9

The Secretary

It might be thought that the duties of the Secretary would fall outside the scope of a work of this nature. And indeed, they largely do. The office of Secretary is generally held by a Past Master, and is principally concerned with the administration of the affairs of the Lodge. However, the Secretary does have one part to play in the ritual, during the ceremony of Installation; and there are also a number of observations which may be made in relation to certain procedural matters.

In the ceremony of Installation the attention of the Master Elect, if he is not already an Installed Master, is directed to the Secretary for the reading of the Ancient Charges and Regulations. When the Master Elect turns towards the Secretary's table, the Secretary rises and reads those Charges, at the end of which he sits. He does not salute the Worshipful Master either before or after reading. If he finds himself unable to refrain from saluting, he should at least remember – as some Secretaries do not – that the Lodge is then open in the second degree, and not in the first.

The wording of the eleventh of those Charges was amended in 1986 in order to restore it very nearly to its original form and now reads:

"11. You admit that it is not in the power of any Man or Body of Men to make any Alteration or Innovation in the Body of Masonry without the consent first obtained of the Grand Lodge."

Over twenty years after the change it might not be thought necessary to make special mention of this point, but there are still

Lodges where the Secretary insists on reading out the Charges from one of the larger print copies of the Book of Constitutions (which have not been produced now for over thirty years) – perhaps the very one that was presented to the Lodge at its Consecration. The Secretary, particularly if he is new, should therefore ensure that he is using an up-to-date version of the Book of Constitutions at this point.

The Secretary has frequent occasion to address the Master in the course of a Lodge meeting, and if he is to be on his feet for any length of time, it is certainly desirable that he does not hold his sign throughout, but salutes smartly at the beginning and the end of what he has to say.

In Emulation Lodge of Improvement the Minutes are not signed by the Master, but after they have been put to the vote, the Secretary stands to order with step and sign when the Master announces "Brother Secretary, the Minutes have been confirmed." This is an exception to the general principle mentioned in Chapter 3, that a Brother does not show the sign when he is addressed by a superior Officer; there is no readily apparent reason for the exception. In a regular Lodge, the Minute Book will normally be taken by the Senior Deacon to the Master for signature at this point, and the Secretary should remember that there is no need for him to turn the Book round before handing it to the Deacon.

When there is a Candidate for Initiation or joining, immediately before the ballot is taken the Secretary is obliged to read from the application form the Candidate's particulars, as required by Rules 159 and 160 of the Book of Constitutions, and the certificate of the Master (see Rule 164); there may also, in certain circumstances, be a Certificate of the Grand Secretary under Rule 164 to be read, or an adverse report under Rule 158 to be brought to the attention of the Lodge. There is no objection to the Secretary, instead of reading the full particulars, referring to the fact that most are set out on the summons, and then reading out the remainder. It is, however, by no means uncommon to find that the Secretary does not read the

Master's Certificate before the ballot, but sends the application form to the Master for the certificate to be signed after the ballot has taken place. This is entirely due to a misreading of what are very clear words both in Rule 164 and on the application form itself. The certificate should always have been signed by the Master before the meeting even begins, indeed preferably before the Candidate has been proposed and seconded in open Lodge, so that it can be read at the proper time.

In a regular Lodge, when the ballot for a Candidate for Initiation takes place at the meeting at which he is to be initiated, it is necessary to inform the Tyler that the ballot has proved favourable, and to ascertain that the Candidate has signed the Declaration required by Rule 162. This duty frequently devolves on the Secretary. If he retires from the Lodge in order to do this, he should not expect to be readmitted by the Inner Guard without going through the procedure of a formal report. There is, of course, no need for the Secretary to witness the signature himself, or for the Declaration Book to be brought into the Lodge. The Secretary (or the Inner Guard on his behalf) can therefore, without passing out of the door, obtain the confirmation of the Tyler that the Declaration is in order. Indeed, the Secretary can quite legitimately merely instruct the Tyler to give the report for the Candidate once he has signed the Declaration, and return at once to his place, thereby minimising the delay to the Lodge proceedings.

From time to time a Lodge is granted a Dispensation, e.g. to change the place or date of a particular meeting, and it will fall to the Secretary to read it. The year date at the end of the Dispensation is customarily given in two forms: e.g. "A.L. 6007, A.D. 2007". Now that Latin is more rarely taught in schools than was once the case, it rather too often happens that the Secretary renders "A.L." incorrectly as "Anno Lucius", rather than "Anno Lucis". The correct pronunciation is either "Anno <u>Loo</u>sis 6007, Anno Domineye 2007" (the "old" or "legal" pronunciation) or "Anno <u>Loo</u>kis 6007, Anno Dominee 2007" (the "new" or "school" pronunciation).

Chapter 10

The Treasurer

The Treasurer shares with the Master and most Tylers the distinction of being elected annually by the members of the Lodge. Historically, he was a man of substance and integrity who could be relied upon to keep the Lodge's funds safe and deliver them up when called for. The task of keeping the financial records of the Lodge generally devolved on the Secretary. More recently, however, the nature of the office has changed, and Treasurers tend now to be elected rather for their skill in book-keeping.

In Emulation Lodge of Improvement, the office of Treasurer is held by a Brother of distinction within the Craft as a whole. The names of several Grand Directors of Ceremonies and Provincial Grand Masters are to be found in the list of those who have served in this capacity. The office in this particular instance is akin to that of President or Patron, being a virtual sinecure, but paradoxically corresponds at least as closely to the original concept as does the modern office in a regular Lodge.

The Treasurer has no duties of a ritual nature to perform. His office is, however, undoubtedly an important one, and he therefore deserves this chapter to himself.

Chapter 11

The Wardens

As in the case of the Deacons, it is convenient to deal with certain preliminary matters which affect both Wardens before considering their duties separately.

Despite their relatively high rank among the Officers of a Lodge, the Wardens have ritual duties significantly less onerous than those of the Deacons, and a great deal less onerous than those of the Master. They will be well advised, if they have not already done so, to utilise the breathing space these two offices afford in order to learn the Master's work.

It is the Master and his two Wardens who rule the Lodge, and as such all three are entitled to attend the Quarterly Communications of Grand Lodge, and, in a Metropolitan Area, Province or District, the meetings of the Metropolitan, Provincial or District Grand Lodge also. When so doing, the Wardens must wear the collars and jewels of their respective offices. They should note, however, that these are the only occasions when they are permitted to do so outside their own Lodge.

On every occasion (save one) that the Master gavels (whether in Lodge or at refreshment) the Wardens repeat his knock or knocks. When they do so they should endeavour to reproduce his rhythm as closely as possible, and also to maintain the same pause between their respective knocks. The only knock given by the Master which is not repeated is the double knock that he gives to summon the Tyler.

The Wardens should remember that, like the Master, they always enter and leave their pedestals in a clockwise direction. Thus the

Junior Warden enters by the east side and leaves by the west, while the Senior Warden enters by the south and leaves by the north.

The Wardens' main ritual duties are in opening and closing the Lodge and in the examination of Candidates, as well as their special duties in the ceremony of Raising. The opening of the Lodge in the three degrees is straightforward, as is the closing in the first and second degrees, and the only matters to which it is necessary to draw attention is that the Wardens must not forget to adjust their columns when the ritual requires, or fail to follow the lead of the Master when "silent" knocks are given. The closing in the third degree is, however, more difficult, and as in a Private Lodge it is frequently omitted, the Lodge being instead resumed in a lower degree, it is worth describing the procedure here in detail.

When the Master calls for the secrets to be communicated to him, the Wardens, still holding the sign, leave their pedestals. The Junior Warden waits at the side of his, while the Senior Warden advances towards the east. As the Senior Warden draws level with him, the Junior Warden moves on to the floor of the Lodge and advances in line abreast with him, preferably without causing him to check in his progress. It is the responsibility of the Senior Warden to select the precise point at which they halt before turning inwards to face each other. This should be a spot roughly equidistant between the Master's pedestal and the Secretary's table. They should avoid standing too far apart, otherwise they may be liable to lose their balance during the communication of the f. ps. o. f..

The Wardens should remember that in what follows the more junior Officer is communicating the secrets to the more senior, and therefore the latter should not anticipate the movements of the former. Having halted, they turn inwards and come into the step. The Junior Warden then takes a further step and extends his hand to the Senior Warden. He then gives the p.g. leading from the second to the third degree, which the Senior Warden returns; the Senior Warden should wait for the g..p to be communicated to him before he adjusts his own hand. They raise their right hands aloft, and the

Junior Warden whispers the p.w.. They disengage, returning immediately to the step and sign. The Junior Warden then takes a further
short step and gives the first three signs of the third degree. Having
recovered, he communicates the f. ps. o. f.. Once again the Senior
Warden should wait to receive each from the Junior before giving it
himself. The Junior Warden whispers the word and they disengage,
going straight back into the step and the sign. The Junior Warden
salutes, turns about, preferably (but not necessarily) by the right, and
returns to his pedestal. Meanwhile the Senior Warden gains the mid-
line of the Lodge, turns east and, without waiting for the Junior
Warden to reach his pedestal, immediately takes a step and addresses
the Master. He then communicates the secrets, just as they were
communicated to him, except that the words are given aloud. They
disengage, and regain the step and sign. The Senior Warden salutes,
turns about (preferably by the right) simultaneously with the Master,
and returns to his pedestal.

The greater part of the work of the Wardens consists in examining
the Candidate. This is fairly straightforward, but Wardens should
bear in mind the following points. First, most of their questions are
addressed to the Candidate himself, even though the answers may be
dictated by the Deacon, and therefore the Warden should look at the
Candidate as he speaks, and not at the Deacon. Secondly, the
Warden must take a step before receiving the Tn. and Wd. of either
degree, but the Senior Warden need not take a step before receiving
the p.g and p.w.. Thirdly, just as in the third degree closing, the
Warden should wait for the Candidate to give a g..p before he
returns it himself.

When the Tracing Board is explained in the second degree
ceremony, the Wardens remain standing in their places so that they
are able to knock at the appropriate point.

In the ceremony of Raising, the Wardens have charge of the
Candidate for a part of the time. When summoned by the Master,
each takes the emblem of his office from its place on his pedestal, and
they advance together to the east, the Junior Warden waiting for the

Senior to draw level with him, as in the third degree closing. Though both will have to step on the s...t as they advance together, they should avoid stepping on the g...e itself. They then with the inside hand simultaneously tap the corresponding Deacon on his inside shoulder and advance into the spaces created by the Deacons stepping to the side. The line thus formed should be held momentarily, and therefore they should not start to take hold of the Candidate until the Deacons have turned outwards to return to their places.

Each Warden then takes one of the Candidate's arms, and the Junior Warden directs him to cross his right foot over the left. In what follows, the Wardens should be at pains to synchronise their actions with the Master's words, and the Junior Warden should not forget to remind the Candidate, if it should be necessary, to recross his feet at the appropriate points. Each of the Wardens in turn, after he has wielded his emblem will need to dispose of it temporarily. A pocket may afford a suitable place, but there is then a risk that the Warden will forget that it is there; it may be best to tuck it under the belt of the apron. When the Candidate is lowered, the Junior Warden should whisper to him to stay rigid. To maintain proper control of the Candidate and minimise the risk of accident each Warden will be well advised to grasp the Candidate's wrist with his own outside hand, whilst sliding his inside hand up the Candidate's arm to support him at the shoulder. Having lowered him, leaving his hands by his sides, each takes up a position beyond the head of the g...e, preferably just to the west of the s...t.

Each Warden when he is asked to endeavour to raise the Candidate advances by the shortest route to a point level with the Candidate's knees, turns, stepping across so that he straddles the Candidate, and raises the latter's right hand about four inches with his own left hand in order to apply the g..p. Having slipped it, he then lowers the Candidate's hand gently to his side, steps back across, returns to his place by the shortest route, turns and makes his report to the Master. When the Candidate is raised, the Wardens assist in the lifting, and a warning from the Junior Warden at this point to stay rigid will do no harm. It is the Senior Warden's responsibility to ensure that the Candidate's left hand and arm are correctly placed once he has been raised. The Wardens resume their seats when so instructed, not forgetting to replace their respective emblems of office.

As sometimes quite senior Freemasons allow themselves to get unduly exercised at the prospect of a Warden's chair being temporarily vacant, it is proper to make it clear that in Emulation working there is no need to fill a Warden's chair if he leaves it temporarily to perform some duty (except, of course, to occupy another chair or office for the time being), provided that he remains within the Lodge. A moment's thought will show that this is actually prescribed in the ritual of the third degree.

The Wardens have little part to play in the procedural duties of the Lodge, and the only observation which I would make is that in Emulation they do not stand on the Risings. If there is an outgoing procession, they will take their places in it as directed by the Director of Ceremonies, but they should halt at the Master's pedestal to allow the Director of Ceremonies to escort the Master to his place behind the Deacons, before closing up.

Chapter 12

The Junior Warden

This is generally the fourth of the junior offices held by a Brother during his progress towards the Chair. As has already been observed, the ritual duties of the office are relatively undemanding. It is therefore at this point in his Masonic career that a Brother should start seriously to learn the work of the Master – if he has not already done so – in order to do full justice to that office when he comes to occupy the Chair.

The Junior Warden should ensure that he is thoroughly familiar with the general matters dealt with in the preceding Chapter, which embrace the greater part of his duties.

When the Junior Warden addresses the Master or the Inner Guard, he should stand square, facing north, and turn only his head towards the Brother whom he is addressing.

In opening the Lodge in the first degree, at the beginning he addresses the Inner Guard by name, but just afterwards when addressing the Master he uses neither the latter's name nor his Office; the report is simply "The Lodge is properly tyled", given without step or sign. In opening the Lodge in the other degrees and in closing in all of them, he gives the sign when he reports "Worshipful Master, the Lodge is properly (or close) tyled." In every case he should be careful not to give the knocks until the Inner Guard has fully discharged his sign. Like the Inner Guard, he should studiously avoid giving undue emphasis to the word "is".

When the Lodge is finally closed the formula used by the Junior Warden in Emulation Lodge of Improvement is "And it is closed accordingly, until Friday evening next, at the hour of six-fifteen." In a regular Lodge a slightly different formula is necessary, but the precise wording is a matter for individual Lodges. The current edition of the Emulation Ritual gives two alternatives, but these are not exhaustive of the possibilities.

A late arrival will be announced by the Inner Guard after the Tyler has given the knocks of the degree in which the Lodge is then open. The Junior Warden gives a single knock in reply; he does not say anything. It is not necessary for the Junior Warden to look first to the Master for approval; he has quite sufficient authority of his own to despatch the Inner Guard to ascertain the identity of the latecomer. The Junior Warden should bear in mind that the Inner Guard is likely to be less experienced than himself, and may therefore be liable to announce a report at an inopportune moment. He should therefore be ready, when he hears the Tyler knock, to signal discreetly to the Inner Guard that the time is or is not right for the report to be announced. The same procedure is adopted when the Candidate returns to the Lodge after restoring himself to his personal comfort, though it is, of course, unlikely that the time will be other than opportune for the report to taken immediately.

In the ceremony of Initiation but in neither of the others, the Junior Warden gavels before standing with step and sign to announce the report to the Master; in the other degrees he immediately stands. In all three degrees, the Junior Warden remains standing to order until he receives his instruction from the Master, whereupon he discharges his sign and sits before addressing the Inner Guard.

The method of examining the Candidate has already been dealt with in the previous chapter, as has the greater part of the procedure in the third degree. In connection with the latter, there are, however, two matters which affect the Junior Warden in particular. In the course of the narrative, the Junior Warden wields the P.R.. When he does so, he employs a glancing movement, sweeping from front to back, in order to suit his action to the words. Subsequently, when the Candidate is lowered to the ground, if a cushion is provided for the Candidate's head – as is the case in Emulation Lodge of Improvement

– it is the responsibility of the Junior Warden to ensure that it is correctly placed.

The Junior Warden has one other ritual duty in the Lodge, which is mentioned at his investiture. It is he who calls the Brethren from labour to refreshment and from refreshment to labour. He should therefore ensure that he is familiar with the brief formula employed for the purpose of calling off and calling on. It is not unknown for a Junior Warden who has otherwise performed his duties in an exemplary fashion, to be taken completely unawares when the Master wishes to call the Lodge off.

At the dinner, the Junior Warden has few duties, but it is perhaps worth observing that in most Lodges, particularly outside London, it is the Junior Warden who proposes the toast to the visitors.

Chapter 13

The Senior Warden

This is generally the fifth of the junior offices held by a Brother during his progress towards the Chair. The Senior Warden should ensure that he is thoroughly familiar with the general matters dealt with in Chapter 11, which, as in the case of the Junior Warden, cover the greater part of his duties.

Although the ritual duties of the office are not unduly heavy, there are one or two points to which the Senior Warden should pay careful attention, especially in the opening and closing.

In opening the Lodge in the first degree, the Senior Warden's reply to the Master's first question to him is "To see that none but Masons are present." In opening the Lodge in the other two degrees, and in closing in all of them, the answer is "To see that the Brethren appear to order as Masons" (or "Craftsmen" or "Master Masons"). It is important to get the words right at this point. Similarly, in both opening and closing in the first degree, the Senior Warden is asked why he is placed in the West, but his answer is slightly different in each case. It is a mark of a competent Senior Warden that he correctly distinguishes the one from the other. In Emulation Lodge of Improvement, the question "The Master's place?" is addressed to the Senior Warden, and is answered by him, as is the succeeding question. In many Lodges, however, these are addressed to, and answered by, the Immediate Past Master. In the act of closing in the second degree the Senior Warden commonly makes a pause between "close" and "this Fellow Crafts' Lodge" to allow the first part of the sign to be discharged; such a pause is unnecessary and produces a stilted effect; the Senior

Warden should deliver the words at an even tempo and synchronise his actions with them.

The procedure for examining the Candidate has already been dealt with in Chapter 11. The Senior Warden should not, however, forget that if immediately afterwards he has to present the Candidate to the Master, he should remain standing. When he presents the Candidate, he should raise the latter's hand only to, or a little above, shoulder height.

When he invests the Candidate, the Senior Warden secures the badge on the Candidate before he starts to address him. In the second and third degrees, he should remove the badge of the lower degree before investing the Candidate with that of the higher; the convolutions which some Senior Wardens go through in order to fasten the new badge before the old is removed are both unnecessary and undignified. The Senior Warden takes hold of the lower right-hand corner (from the Candidate's point of view) of the badge with his left hand, and retains his hold on it until he has finished speaking. In the first degree the Senior Warden strikes the apron with his right hand at the word "badge", and not at the word "that" which precedes it. The first and second degree badge is generally fastened with strings, but that of a Master Mason has an adjustable belt and buckle. It is prudent on the part of the Senior Warden to check before the meeting begins that the requisite apron is at his pedestal and in the case of the third degree that the belt has been adjusted to the Candidate's dimensions.

The greater part of the procedure in the third degree has already been dealt with in Chapter 11. There are, however, two matters which affect the Senior Warden in particular. In the course of the narrative, the Senior Warden wields the level. Whereas the Junior Warden employs a glancing movement with the P.R., the Senior Warden delivers a straightforward blow (a light one, please!) in suiting his action to the words. Subsequently, when the Candidate is raised it is the responsibility of the Senior Warden to ensure that his left arm and hand are correctly placed.

Chapter 14

The Master Elect

This is not, strictly speaking, an office so much as a situation, since the individual concerned is for part of the time generally still the Senior Warden, and for the remainder of the time Worshipful Master. However, to avoid splitting the remarks which relate to the Master Elect between two separate chapters, it is convenient to give him a chapter to himself.

In Emulation Lodge of Improvement the ceremony of Installation is always worked in full, as though the Master Elect were being installed for the first time, though of necessity the Brother acting as such will be an Installed Master. It should therefore be borne in mind that the suggestions made in the ritual for abbreviating the ceremony if the Master Elect is already an Installed Master cannot reflect the practice of Emulation Lodge of Improvement itself.

Before the ceremony of Installation begins, Installed Masters are placed in the Wardens' chairs. The Master Elect should at this point remove the collar and jewel of his office, as it will interrupt the smooth flow of the ceremony at a later point if he is still wearing them.

When, after his presentation, the Master Elect's attention is directed to the Secretary, he turns to face the latter, and at the end of the first of the Ancient Charges he takes a step and gives the sign of F., which he drops (not cuts) immediately, but remains with his feet in the step. He gives and drops the sign after each of the succeeding charges, and at their conclusion, he turns to face the Master once more.

When the Installing Master directs him to advance to the pedestal, the Master Elect may move either after the word "pedestal" or at the end of the sentence, though the latter is preferable. If it is the practice of the Lodge to wear gloves, the Master Elect should not forget to remove at least his right glove at this point. If he is already an Installed Master, he is expected to recite the obligation which follows; otherwise it is dictated to him by the Installing Master in the usual way.

Near the conclusion of the Inner Working, the newly installed Master invests the Immediate Past Master using the form of words which is printed in the ritual, but which is sometimes overlooked by the Master Elect when preparing for his Installation.

In the course of the ceremony the Lodge is closed in the third and second degrees, and in Emulation Lodge of Improvement this is always done in full when the Installation is worked (see Chapter 19). In many Lodges it is the practice to save time by resuming in the lower degree, but where it is customary to close in full, the Master Elect should ensure that both he and the Brethren acting as Wardens are conversant with the manner of doing so, as this is part of the Installation ceremony and will reflect upon himself.

When the perambulations and the presentation of the W.Ts. in the three degrees have been completed, the Installing Master presents the Master Elect with the Warrant of the Lodge. In some workings the Master Elect stands at this point, but in Emulation he does *not* do so.

The only other ritual duty which the Master Elect – or, more properly, the newly installed Master – has to perform during the ceremony of Installation is the investing of his Officers. Just as it is the mark of a competent Senior Warden that he correctly distinguishes the opening of the Lodge from the closing, so it is the mark of a good Master Elect that he uses the correct formula in investing his Officers. It is fair to say that this particular piece of work is one of the most difficult to get right in all of the Craft ritual, because the formulae employed for the various Officers are all very similar, yet all slightly different. He should remember that the Wardens are *his* ("I appoint you my Senior/Junior Warden"), while the other Officers are those of the *Lodge* ("I appoint you Secretary of the Lodge"). He invests the Senior Warden and Treasurer with the *insignia*, the Junior Warden with the *collar and jewel*, and every other Officer with the *jewel* of his office. Finally he should not forget to give the double knock at the appropriate point to summon the Tyler for investiture. The Master Elect who invests all his Officers in exactly the right words is fully entitled to take some satisfaction in his achievement, and will certainly have signalled to his Brethren that they may expect a good year under his Mastership.

For completeness, I should add that, although it is not Emulation working, in some Lodges (particularly Installed Masters' Lodges) it is the custom not to use the full formula to invest those Officers who are Past Masters, on the basis that they are already fully familiar with their duties.

For many newly Installed Masters the after-proceedings may be no less alarming a prospect than the work in the Lodge. The Master Elect will therefore, if he is prudent, make himself familiar with the final section of Chapter 15.

The Worshipful Master

There is no higher, and, theoretically, no more important, office in a Lodge than that of the Worshipful Master. Upon him devolves the responsibility for working the ceremonies during his year of office, or for arranging for others to undertake the work. In addition to these ritual duties, there are many others that devolve upon him, but they are outside the scope of this book. However, the fact that those duties exist makes it even more desirable that the Master should have made himself familiar with the ritual work before he reaches the Chair, as the time available for learning at that late stage is diminished by the competing pressures.

It goes without saying that the Master should be conversant with the matters dealt with in Chapter 3, and if possible he should attend regularly, if he has not previously done so, at a Lodge of Instruction, as it is by actual practice that the way to deliver the ceremonies is best learned.

Whereas in the previous chapters it has been necessary to deal at some length with the actions and movements which accompany the words of the ritual, in the case of the Master these are in general more straightforward, because of his largely static situation. I have therefore felt able to devote rather more space to hints and mnemonics, which I hope will be of assistance to Masters in remembering the correct sequence and wording of the ritual, as well as its better delivery.

Most of these hints will be dealt with at the appropriate point in the commentary, but there is one which has no particularly obvious place, and therefore I deal with it here. I have already mentioned in

Chapter 3 that the word "upon" is very sparingly used in the Emulation ritual, and is limited to three instances only, all of them in the Master's work. There is one occurrence in the first degree, at the "charity test": "Indeed I shall immediately proceed to put your principles in some measure to the test, by calling *upon* you to exercise that virtue which may justly be denominated the distinguishing characteristic of a Freemason's heart; I mean Charity." The word does not occur at all in the second degree. It occurs once in the third, at the very beginning of the Exhortation: "Having entered *upon* the solemn obligation of a Master Mason". Finally, it occurs once in the Installation, during the Address to the Worshipful Master: "Forcibly impress *upon* them the dignity and high importance of Masonry". On every other occasion in Emulation working, the word "on" is used.

Opening and Closing the Lodge

The method of opening and closing in the three degrees is very adequately detailed in the Emulation Ritual, but the following matters are worthy of attention.

In opening the Lodge in any degree, the first question addressed to the Junior Warden is "What is the first care?" whereas in closing it is "What is the constant care?" When the Junior Warden subsequently reports back that the Lodge is properly, or close, tyled, the Master should be careful not to address the next question to the Senior Warden until the Junior Warden has fully discharged his sign (if any), to the point of recovery where appropriate.

In opening the Lodge in the first degree, the Master should remember that until the Brethren have come to order, thereby proving themselves Masons, he addresses each of the Wardens by his name, and not by his office. Thereafter, the general rule is that when there is an interchange between the Master and one or both Wardens which continues without a break, he addresses them respectively as "Brother Senior Warden" and "Brother Junior Warden" only in the first remark addressed to each. The exception is when he addresses them in that manner to ask them their respective places and duties. (A little thought will show that the exception is necessary in order to maintain the principle of naming each Officer in the course of asking his place and situation.) In the remaining openings and closings, the general rule holds good.

In Emulation working, the last two questions in the first degree opening ("The Master's place?" and "Why is he placed there?") are addressed to the Senior Warden, and not as in some other workings to the Immediate Past Master.

In Emulation Lodge of Improvement, the Master delivers the prayers himself, as there is no Chaplain. However, in many, if not most, regular Lodges a Chaplain is appointed, and he will therefore deliver the prayers. These begin, except for that in the third degree opening (which the Master frequently delivers himself, as it is so short) at the words "Let us ....". The usual practice is for the Master to deliver the few words which precede each prayer himself, and for the Chaplain to take up the words at the start of the prayer. This is, however, not a matter on which there can strictly be an Emulation view; the main consideration here is to ensure a smooth change-over between the Master and the Chaplain, and it is at least prudent for them to agree a common policy in advance. When the Master delivers the prayers himself, he may find the keyword "OPHelia" helpful in remembering the order of the words in the first degree opening ("... begun in *order*, be conducted in *peace* and closed in *harmony*"). Similarly in closing, the initials of a well-known high street store should ensure that "moral" and "social" are given in the correct order.

In the second degree opening the Master should deliver the words "duly open on the Sq." without any pause; the sign should be discharged in two movements, but the action can easily be synchronised without distorting the flow of the words.

Occasionally in the third degree opening one hears the Master, perhaps anxious to deliver the ritual with *meaning*, ask the Senior Warden "Whither directing *your* course?" This is even less legitimate than the Inner Guard or Junior Warden reporting "the Lodge *is* properly tyled". In fact it makes nonsense of the passage since both Wardens are figuratively travelling in the same direction (as is quite clear from the rest of the opening and from the third degree closing) and emphasising "*your*" implies that the Senior and Junior Wardens are travelling in different directions. The important words in the question are *directing* and *course*.

It is a curious fact that in the third degree opening, the Master quite commonly forgets to ask the Junior Warden the question "How came they lost?", though he hardly ever forgets any of the other questions. I have observed this not only at Emulation Lodge of Improvement itself but also at many private Lodges, whether they work Emulation, or some other ritual. The Master should therefore be particularly on his guard against the commission of this particular error. At the end of the third degree opening, the Master must remember that before giving the G. or R. sign he must allow the Inner Guard (and the Junior Deacon as well, if he has the duty of changing the Tracing Boards) time not only to return to his place but also to take a step.

When the secrets are communicated in closing the Lodge in the third degree, the Master effectively duplicates the actions of the Senior Warden when the latter receives them from the Junior Warden. He should ensure that he does not stand too far away from the Senior Warden, as the risk of overbalancing is thereby minimised, and as he is receiving the secrets from the Senior Warden, he should not anticipate the latter at any of the points.

Before the Lodge is finally closed (except at an emergency meeting), the Master rises three times, normally in the first degree – though the practice in Emulation Lodge of Improvement is generally otherwise (see Chapter 19). The Master should time his action to suit his words; that is to say, he should not start to rise until he has started speaking. Brethren should note that in Emulation working the Master rises to *ask if* etc., and that he gives only the name of the Lodge, without the number.

At an emergency meeting of a Lodge (for which, of course, a dispensation will have been previously obtained) the Book of Constitutions provides that no business shall be transacted except such as is mentioned on the summons convening the meeting (see Rule 140). It therefore necessarily follows that there can be no risings on such an occasion, since they exist only as the means of introducing other business.

The Ceremonies

Apart from the ceremony of Installation, which is dealt with separately in the next chapter, the ceremonies follow a very similar structural pattern, of which the ceremony of Passing affords the basic example. It is true, however, that the third degree displays a number of significant points of difference, probably to be accounted for by its late date of development; and the first degree also contains a number of embellishments; but the common features are still very noticeable.

The ceremonies of Passing and Raising each begin with an examination of the Candidate's knowledge of the preceding degree, followed by entrustment with the p.g. and p.w.. For obvious reasons there is no parallel in the ceremony of Initiation. The Master begins by announcing the item of business, and asking Entered Apprentices (or Fellow Crafts) other than the Candidate to retire. This last is not done in Emulation Lodge of Improvement, as only Master Masons can be present. (In some Lodges purporting to work Emulation, Entered Apprentices – or Fellow Crafts – other than the Candidate are only asked to retire after the Candidate has been conducted to the pedestal after he has answered the test questions. There are arguments both for and against such a practice: on the one hand, allowing other Entered Apprentices – or Fellow Crafts – to be present during the test questions will help to familiarise them with the answers they will be called to give when their turn comes; on the other, it makes for a distracting break in the ceremony while they leave the Lodge.) The Junior or Senior Deacon, as the case may be, then leads the Candidate to a position at the edge of the floor to the north of the Senior Warden's pedestal. Only then does the Master begin the ceremony with the words "Brethren, Brother ..... is this evening a Candidate ...".

At the conclusion of the test questions, the Candidate, now at the north side of the Master's pedestal, is asked two further questions before entrustment. The Master does not rise to communicate the p.g. and p.w. until after the words "seek to be admitted". He does not take a step. He completes the placing of the Candidate's thumb before he places his own. As soon as he has returned the Candidate's hand to the Deacon he sits. When the Lodge is opened or resumed in the higher degree, he gives the knocks "silently" so that they are audible only within the Lodge. It is not necessary or, for that matter, desirable for him to reverse the head of his gavel in order to do this.

None of the ceremonies calls for any comment until the direction to the Inner Guard to admit the Candidate in due form. The Master must pause at this point to allow the Inner Guard to discharge his sign, before he calls on the Deacons. Once the Candidate has been admitted, in the first degree the Master puts a question to him before desiring him to kneel; in the other degrees he desires him to kneel as soon as he has advanced to the kneeling stool as a Mason or a Fellow Craft, as the case may be. He should be at pains not to gavel until the Candidate has finished kneeling, and (except in the first degree) has shown the sign of R.; in the third degree it is not always easy to determine when the Candidate has done so, and the Master should therefore err on the side of delay. Having gavelled, he should set an example to the other Brethren by not standing until the Junior Warden has gavelled. In Emulation Lodge of Improvement the Master delivers the prayer himself; in many regular Lodges this will be done by the Chaplain. At the conclusion of the prayer, in the first degree there is a further question before the Candidate rises; in the other degrees the Master asks the Candidate to rise immediately he has dropped the sign of R.. As soon as the Candidate has risen, the Master and the other Brethren sit.

At this point, the Candidate is conducted round the Lodge. There is one perambulation in each degree which he has already received, and one additional perambulation, preceded by an announcement from the Master, for the degree to which he is about to be admitted. This means that in the first degree the Master's announcement follows almost as soon as he has resumed his seat. He must, however, allow the Senior Deacon to draw aside the kneeling stool before he gavels.

At the conclusion of the perambulations, the Senior Warden presents the Candidate to the Master. In the second and third degrees the latter immediately gives directions to be passed on to the Deacon(s); in the first degree, however, there are first some questions to be answered. The Master must not start on those questions until the Junior Deacon has again taken charge of the Candidate and the Senior Warden has resumed his seat.

When the Candidate has advanced to the Master's pedestal and knelt after giving his assent to taking the Obligation, in the first degree the Master must place the Candidate's right hand on the V.S.L. and position the Cs. in his left. This last is not difficult, but is not always carried out in the most efficient manner. The Cs. used are a spare pair – those from the third degree W.Ts. will do if no other are available – and *on no account* should the pair on the V.S.L. be employed for this purpose. In view of the risk of the Candidate injuring himself, some care should be exercised in their positioning. The best method is for the Master to open the legs of the Cs. to a right angle, place one leg in the Candidate's clenched left fist, with the little finger near the pivot, and place his left thumb so that it extends along the leg towards, but a fraction of an inch short of, the point. By bringing the Candidate's thumb up to his left breast, the Cs. can be accurately and safely positioned. The other leg of the Cs. will, of course, hang down perpendicularly, so that the Cs. will be as stable as possible. The Master may find that he has to stand in order to carry out this procedure satisfactorily. If such is the case, he must resume his seat before he gavels, which on this occasion he should do *quietly*, so as not to startle the Candidate and perhaps cause him to injure himself.

In the second degree at this point, the Master has only to remember that he must allow the Junior Deacon to apply the Sq., before he gavels. In the third degree there is not even that complication.

The administering of the Obligation is one of the most difficult parts of any ceremony. The Master is unable to take it at his own pace, and the Candidate's – and even his own – nervousness can often cause difficulty. This is the one part of the ceremony which, more than any other, the Master must know really well. He must break the Obligation into phrases which are not too long for the Candidate to repeat accurately, and he must dictate each phrase clearly and distinctly. In the case of the first degree Obligation, the phrases will probably need to be very short indeed – four or five words at most. But even in the second and third degrees large chunks are better avoided. In addition, it is preferable, and certainly more elegant, if the Master breaks the phrases in accordance with the sense, rather than arbitrarily. Thus "I further solemnly promise / that I will not write those secrets" is better than "I further solemnly promise that / I will not write those secrets"; and both are better than "I further solemnly / promise that I will / not write those secrets". It may be found a useful tip for the Master in preparing himself for a ceremony to rehearse the Obligation by repeating each phrase twice. This serves a dual purpose; it gets him into the habit of breaking the Obligation into short phrases, and it accustoms him to the check in the onward flow caused by having to pause for the repetition of each phrase.

Two specific examples of sensible breaking up of the words may be helpful as an illustration. In the first degree obligation, in a certain part the appropriate break points are "....or otherwise them delineate / on anything / moveable or immoveable / under....". In the third degree obligation when dealing with the f. ps. o. f. it will be most effective if the Master makes the individual breaks coincide with the naming of the individual ps.: "That my h. / given etc ...... that my ft. / shall etc." and so on.

In the course of the Obligation, the Master at the words "do hereby and hereon" touches first the Candidate's hand and then the V.S.L.. He uses his left hand to do so and not, as is sometimes seen, the right, which should be otherwise engaged. He should touch hand and V.S.L. as the Candidate repeats the words, and not as he himself dictates them, and it is preferable if he breaks the phrases: "do hereby / and hereon".

At the end of the Obligation, the Master gives the lead to the Brethren in cutting the sign. Before requiring the Candidate to seal the Obligation, the Master must himself in the first degree remove the Cs. from the Candidate's left hand, and in the second degree must allow the Junior Deacon to remove the Sq. and return it to the Senior Deacon.

In the first degree, the Candidate is now restored to light. Having given the command to the Junior Deacon, the Master waits until the latter catches his eye to indicate that the bow is untied and he is ready to remove the h.....k, and then raises his gavel. He moves it first left, then right, and finally brings it down on the pedestal or sounding block. If he has performed this procedure properly, the clap from the Brethren will be simultaneous with the sounding of his gavel. Unfortunately this is not always the case, and when it is not, the fault almost always lies with the Master. The three movements of the gavel must be made positively, visibly and rhythmically, since they set the time for the Brethren. The Master should see himself here in the role of the conductor of an orchestra, using his gavel as the baton; he gives two free beats to set the time, and then brings in his players together on the third. If the players cannot see the beat clearly, or if he varies the interval between the beats, unanimity is unlikely to be achieved. Masters often seem to lose their nerve on the final downward beat, with the result that the clap precedes the gavel.

In explaining the three great lights, the Master should on no account in the second and third degrees adjust the Sq. and Cs. to show their relative positions.

After the explanation of the three great lights, the Master raises the Candidate by simply taking him by the right hand. He does not make any attempt to give the g..p of the degree. He places the Candidate's hand in that of the Deacon and sits. At this point, although the first and second degrees continue to run in parallel, the third diverges and will therefore be dealt with separately below.

In the first and second degrees, the Candidate is conducted to the north side of the pedestal in readiness for the entrustment with the secrets of the degree. In the first degree, however, there is an additional feature – the explanation of the three lesser lights and the "three great dangers". In explaining the former, the Master will be well advised to avoid pointing; for while there can be no actual harm in indicating the three lights, it is all too easy for him to point again when he explains their significance, generally with unfortunate results.

The Master, in explaining the "three great dangers", at the appropriate moment, presents the p....d as close as may be to the Candidate's breast without actually touching him. He then replaces it on the pedestal, resheathing it if necessary, and waits to receive the c.t. from the Junior Deacon before proceeding with the next words, during which it is immaterial whether he draws the n...e or not. In Emulation Lodge of Improvement the c.t. (an imaginary one) is handed to the member of the precepting Committee acting as Immediate Past Master.

When the Master directs the Candidate to take the step, he must ensure that the latter does so correctly, and should not continue with the words "That is the first/second regular step" until the Candidate has come into the correct position. At this point the Candidate is in the charge of the Master, whose responsibility it is to see that he does what is required of him, without assistance from the Deacon unless it is absolutely necessary. The Master does not rise until he is about to start the explanation of the sign; i.e. in the first degree after

"They consist of a sign, Tn. and Wd." and in the second degree after "in this degree the sign is of a threefold nature". He must not forget to take a step as soon as he stands.

The actual communication of the sign(s) rarely causes difficulty. There are, however, two points to be remembered when the allusion of the sign is explained. First, immediately before he demonstrates the sign it is almost universally the practice for the Master to whisper "copy me" to the Candidate; these words should on no account be spoken aloud, and if possible should be mouthed only. Secondly, it is of great importance that the Master uses the correct tense – "would rather *have had* ..." – to emphasise the historical and symbolical nature of the penalty. In the second degree he must not forget also to explain the full penalty (N.B. "r....ous bs. o. t. a. o. d.....ing bts. o. t. f."). The points apply with equal force in the ceremony of Raising, though at a different part of the ceremony.

In explaining the Tn., the Master adjusts the Candidate's thumb before placing his own, as in the entrustment before Passing and Raising. In the exchange which follows, he should remember that it is the Candidate, and not the Deacon, whom he is examining, and should therefore keep his eyes on the former throughout the examination. At the conclusion of the explanation of the derivation of the word, he returns the Candidate's hand to the Deacon and sits.

There is little of difficulty in the procedure at the investiture of the Candidate, though the Master must not forget to strike his own badge (in the first degree) when all the other Brethren do so, and to allow the Deacon to take up a position on the Candidate's right before adding his own further address. The charges delivered to the Candidate after he has been placed in the north-east or south-east part of the Lodge call for little comment. In the case of the former, however, the Master should take note of the rare occurrence of the word "upon" and the fact that there is a comma between "sister" and "Mercy". He must also allow the Junior Deacon to return to the

Candidate's side following the "charity test" before he continues "I congratulate you on the honourable sentiments ..."

The W.Ts. will have been placed by the Immediate Past Master in readiness for their explanation, and there will be no occasion for the Master to touch them. In Emulation Lodge of Improvement, they are laid out on the pedestal, between the V.S.L. and the Master, but in most regular Lodges it will be found more practicable for them to be laid out on the left-hand side of the pedestal, probably on the lid of the box in which they are kept. During the explanation, it is sufficient for the Master to point to each of the W.Ts. in turn, and on no account should he actually handle them.

In the second degree, the Candidate retires immediately after the explanation of the W.Ts.; in the first degree, he must first be shown the Warrant and receive a copy of the Book of Constitutions and the By-laws. In Emulation working the Master does not stand in order to show the Warrant to the Candidate, or at any other time when he handles it. This is perhaps a convenient point at which to mention that, although Rule 101 of the Book of Constitutions provides that the Master shall produce the Warrant at every meeting of the Lodge, it is not necessary for him to display it at the beginning of each meeting. "Produce" in the context of Rule 101 means no more than bring out of safe keeping and have available for inspection. So long as the Warrant is physically present inside the Lodge Room the Master has discharged his duty under the Rule (see also "Information for the Guidance of Members of the Craft").

In the first degree, the Charge delivered on the return of the new Entered Apprentice is entirely straightforward, and calls for no comment at all. In the second degree, the Master waits until the Senior Deacon has conducted the Candidate to the Tracing Board and the Junior Deacon has joined them before he rises and makes his own way to the east of the Tracing Board to deliver the Explanation. He receives the Junior Deacon's wand, without moving from his own position. It is customary for the Master to use the wand to indicate the various features on the Tracing Board in the course of the Explanation, though it is not essential that all, or indeed any, of the items are pointed out. It has frequently been a matter of debate which is the left-hand P., and which the right. There is no official Emulation view on this question, which has exercised many distinguished biblical and Masonic scholars, but for convenience the convention has been adopted that in Emulation Lodge of Improvement the Master should indicate the P. which is on his own left or right as he stands facing west.

Towards the end of the Explanation there is reference to certain Hebrew characters depicted by the letter G. Where, as is the case in Emulation Lodge of Improvement, the Tracing Board illustrates both, it should be the letter G which the Master indicates at the appropriate moment (though it is not positively wrong to point to the Hebrew characters). He then waits while a Past Master and the Wardens gavel. He must not immediately give the sign of R., but must wait until he has said the words "denoting G."; he then holds the sign (with the wand resting in the crook of his right shoulder) until the conclusion of the Explanation, when he drops the sign and returns the wand to the Junior Deacon.

Reverting now to the third degree, we left off at that part of the ceremony where the Candidate has just been raised after his Obligation. The Deacons back him to the foot of the g...e, and the Master delivers the Exhortation. Note the word "upon". At the conclusion of the Exhortation, he summons the Wardens, and waits until both Deacons have resumed their seats and the Candidate has crossed his feet before he proceeds with the ceremony. Many Brethren may be unaware of the useful keyword "SOAP", which is a helpful mnemonic standing for "South", "Opposed", "Accosted", "Posted", as a means of remembering the manner in which the three ruffians confronted H.A.. In the course of that passage, the latter replies at one point that he would rather suffer death than betray etc.. It is all too frequently the case that the Master emphasises the word "death" at this point; yet to do so is quite wrong, for although death is the most serious consequence imaginable, death is the only consequence which has been mentioned and therefore the only consequence in issue; the emphasis should be placed on either "rather" or "suffer", each of which is quite legitimate. At the conclusion of this passage, when the Master himself wields the H.M., he does not stand to do so.

In many Lodges, as soon as the Candidate has been laid on the ground, a passage from the twelfth chapter of the Book of Ecclesiastes is recited. This is *not* Emulation working, but it may be observed that if the custom is followed, the passage should end at verse 7 – "and the spirit shall return unto God who gave it" – and should not include the next verse, the addition of which introduces an unnecessary element of anti-climax.

After the Wardens have made their trials, the Master raises the Candidate with their assistance. Having left his pedestal (by the south side), he proceeds to the foot of the g...e, where he uncrosses the Candidate's right foot, placing it about six inches from the left, and places his own right foot against it. To move the Candidate's left foot back so that his left leg is bent at the knee, although commonly to be seen, is *not* Emulation working, however much it may allegedly (though not actually) facilitate the act of raising. He then steps forward with his left foot, and takes the Candidate by the right hand, ensuring that both he and the Candidate have the thumb and fingers correctly positioned for the first of the f. ps. o. f.. The Master gives a whispered word or a signal to indicate to the Wardens that he is ready, and presses down with his own left foot, swinging backwards at the same time, so that with the assistance of the Wardens the Candidate is lifted to an upright position, as nearly as possible in the position of the f. ps. o. f.. After his brief address to the Candidate, the Master disengages and directs the Wardens to resume their seats, before taking the Candidate by both hands and positioning him a little to the east of the s...t, and about level with the north edge of it, facing south. He himself takes up a corresponding position level with the south edge.

During the Charge the Master may wish to indicate certain visible items; while this is not wrong in Emulation working, it is important that correct references are made. Thus if he points at "that Light which is from above" it should be to the V.S.L. and not upwards towards the ceiling. In the words that follow, Masters frequently fail to punctuate according to the proper sense: it is not "the g...e into which you have just figuratively descended and which..."; it is "the g...e (into which you have just figuratively descended) and which, when....... away, will again receive you....". In other words, it is the figurative g...e, represented on the s...t, and not the s...t itself, which one day will receive .....

After the delivery of the Charge, the Master again takes the Candidate by both hands and swings him round (interposing himself between the Candidate and the pedestal) so that their positions are approximately reversed. In fact both he and the Candidate should be a little to the south of the other's former position. The object of the exercise is to ensure as nearly as possible that when the Candidate has taken the three steps, and the Master has taken one, they will be standing directly in front of the pedestal for the communication of the secrets. The Master should note in this connection that he does not take his own step until the Candidate has stood to order as a Fellow Craft. The first of the signs involves two quite distinct movements, first with the left hand to a point directly in front (the d. and a. s. is supposed to be in front of, and not behind or to the side of, the person giving the sign), and then with the right hand and head (the body does not move). If the Master and Candidate have both given the sign correctly their left hands should be almost touching. The second sign may be given with either the palm or the fingers, though the former is probably the more natural. The third sign is in this instance given by bringing the hand immediately to the left side (see also Chapter 3).

It is preferable that as he communicates the f. ps. o. f. the Master should finish naming each before demonstrating it. When they disengage before the Master explains the f. ps. briefly, both he and the Candidate should resume the step. As soon as the Candidate has repeated both versions of the word, they again disengage, and after the next few words the Master returns immediately to his pedestal (by the north side). He does not wait for the Senior Deacon to take charge of the Candidate.

The investiture of the Candidate presents no problem, and the Traditional History calls for no special comment, except when the first two signs are demonstrated. At that point the Master does not take a step when he stands, but merely demonstrates the signs. The first of these he holds until after the word "sight". After giving the second, he again sits; if he has not done so by then, the word "descended" should give him a reminder.

In Emulation Lodge of Improvement the Immediate Past Master hands the Master a miniature Tracing Board at the appropriate moment, together with the pencil from the set of W.Ts. to enable him to point out the various features to the Candidate. He receives them back again at the end of the explanation.

When he demonstrates all five signs to the Candidate immediately after the explanation of the Tracing Board, the Master *does* take a step, and should wait for the Candidate to so also before starting on the demonstration. The fourth sign is given with the right hand held in the f. o. a s. throughout. In the first of the alternative versions of the fourth sign, the hands are drawn apart as the first of the words is spoken. In the second, the hands are bent back at the wrists so that the palms lie as nearly as possible parallel to the ceiling at the start of the sign. The ceremony concludes with the presentation of the W.Ts..

Procedural and Miscellaneous Matters

If the Lodge is meeting by Dispensation, whether because the meeting is an emergency one, or because the date or venue has been changed, the first item after the Lodge has been opened, and before any business is taken, must be the reading of the Dispensation.

Except when the death of one of the members has occurred since the last meeting, in which case it is customary to deliver a tribute at the end of which the Brethren stand to order, the first item of business at any regular meeting will normally be the reading of the Minutes. At an emergency meeting, however, the Minutes of the last regular meeting must not be read; instead there will be two sets of Minutes for confirmation at the next regular meeting. (In Emulation Lodge of Improvement, the Minutes are taken at a different point in the meeting, immediately after the Lodge has been called back on for the second half of the evening.) In Emulation Lodge of Improvement the Master usually enquires "Brother Secretary, are the Minutes ready?", though in a regular Lodge other formulae such as "Brother Secretary, may we have the Minutes of our last meeting?" are normally used. At the conclusion of the Minutes, the Master announces "Brethren, the Minutes of our last meeting are before you. Those who deem them a correct record and worthy of confirmation will signify the same in the manner usually observed among Masons. (Pause) To the contrary? (Pause) Brother Secretary, the Minutes are confirmed." Again variations in the exact wording are quite permissible. It should be noted that although the full formula is used for the Minutes, in Emulation Lodge of Improvement any further vote is introduced by "Brethren, the proposition is before you. Those in favour. (Pause) To the contrary?"

There is one other matter which may conveniently be dealt with at this point. The Master has a gavel to enable him to keep order. In these days, whatever may have been the case in former times, it is unusual for Lodge proceedings to degenerate into such disorder that the Master will need to gavel in order to obtain the attention of the Brethren. Many Masters, however, are given to using the gavel on almost every occasion on which it could conceivably be appropriate to do so, and even on some on which it is not. In Emulation Lodge of Improvement, the Master does not normally use his gavel except when the ritual expressly requires him to do so. Whilst individual Masters and Lodges are free in this, as in many other matters, to do as they please, it is certainly my own opinion that the repeated use of the gavel is as undesirable as it is unnecessary.

When there is a ballot to be taken, the Master announces "Brother Deacons, there is a ballot." The ballot box is brought by the Senior Deacon to the south side of the pedestal, where the drawers (or at least the "no" drawer) are checked. In Emulation Lodge of Improvement this is done by the member of the Committee acting as Immediate Past Master, but in a regular Lodge it would normally be done by the Master himself. The Master then announces "Brethren, we are about to ballot for Brother (or Mister) ....." If there are two or more Candidates to be balloted for, the announcement will be "Brethren, we are about to ballot for those Brethren whose names have been read by the Secretary. We will take them together, and separately afterwards, if necessary." The Master is the last to receive a token from the Junior Deacon, which he places in the box when the Senior Deacon presents it at the north side of the pedestal. The box is then again presented for examination at the south side, where it is checked as before, and the result announced. The precise formula in use in Emulation Lodge of Improvement is given in Chapter 19. In a regular Lodge it is quite sufficient to announce "Brethren, the ballot is in favour of the Candidate(s)." Masters frequently state that a ballot is unanimous if there is no token in the "no" drawer, but that is not necessarily the case; it may be that one or more members of the Lodge have not voted. In any event it is better to make the announcement in neutral terms on every occasion, so as to avoid embarrassment if there should prove to be one or more black balls cast, in which case the word "unanimous" is clearly inappropriate.

When the ballot is for a joining member, he will normally have retired while it is taken, though it is not essential that he should do so. Once the result of the ballot has been announced to him, assuming it to be in his favour, he must be presented with a copy of the By-laws of the Lodge (see Rule 138 of the Book of Constitutions). It is not, however, necessary that he be presented with a copy of the Book of Constitutions, unless he is joining from another Constitution.

Where a paper ballot is taken in a regular Lodge for the Master and Treasurer, the same procedure with modifications should be adopted, with the Junior Deacon distributing the ballot papers and the Senior Deacon collecting them. If it appears that the ballot is contested, the Master will be well advised to ask the Immediate Past Master or some other Brother of standing in the Lodge to act as scrutineer as he counts the papers. Since 2004, however, Rule 105(a) which regulates the election of Master has provided: "If there be only one nomination and if no other member duly qualified shall have indicated to the Master or Secretary that he wishes to be considered and if no member present calls for a ballot then it shall be permissible for the Master to declare the election in favour of the nominated member; provided that the election shall not be so declared unless notice of the intention so to do and the identity of the sole Brother nominated shall have been given on the summons convening the meeting at which the election is to take place." Rule 112 has also been amended to provide that the Treasurer shall be elected in the same manner as the Master. It is therefore likely that paper ballots will be take place much less frequently in the future. It should be observed, however, that there are several conditions that must be fulfilled in order for the simplified procedure to be used. It is therefore suggested that the Master should proceed as follows. After announcing that the next item is to ballot for the Master he should address the Secretary in some such words as: "Brother Secretary, it appears from the summons that Brother ...... is the only Brother nominated to serve as Master for the ensuing year. Has any other Brother subsequently indicated to you that he wishes to be considered?" On receiving a negative reply from the Secretary, he should ask: "Brethren, neither Brother Secretary nor I have received notice that any other Brother wishes to be considered. Does any member of the Lodge wish to call, nevertheless, for a ballot? (Pause) Then I declare Brother ...... elected as Master for the ensuing year."

It may be helpful to set out the correct pronunciation of certain words which are often found to cause difficulty. Appendix 1 contains a small number of such words.

In Emulation Lodge of Improvement, all of the work allocated in the printed ritual to the Master ("chair work") is carried out by him. However, it is the established practice in many regular Lodges for the Master to "farm out" a number of portions of the chair work. Three reasons are often given for the practice:

(a) it reduces the burden on the Master;
(b) it gives an opportunity of working to Brethren who would not otherwise get such an opportunity; and
(c) it provides variety for the remaining Brethren, who are thus spared having to listen to a single voice doing the chair work throughout the meeting.

The relative importance of these reasons will no doubt vary according to the identity of the Master. There is strong encouragement from the most senior members of the Craft for the farming out of suitable portions of the ritual work for both of reasons (a) and (b). Circumstances vary greatly from Lodge to Lodge, and whereas in some Lodges the policy adopted by the Worshipful Master may be slanted towards allocating work to Past Masters who might otherwise find themselves "on the shelf", in others the emphasis may need to be towards giving work to more junior Brethren who have not yet reached the chair, or even are not on the "ladder" of progressive offices.

If the Chair is temporarily occupied by an Installed Master to whom part or all of a ceremony has been farmed out, the Master takes the seat immediately to the left of the Chair which would otherwise be occupied by the Immediate Past Master. The latter together with the Chaplain (if any) moves a place to the left. The Master does, however, retain the Master's collar and jewel, and the Brother temporarily occupying the Chair is clothed according to his own rank and/or office. The only situation in which the Master's collar and jewel are worn by another Brother is when the Master is actually absent.

The After-Proceedings

The Master presides at dinner as well as in the Lodge, and whilst the after-proceedings are not strictly within the scope of a work such as this, Masters may find a little guidance of some assistance.

If the Lodge is a Hall Stone Lodge, the Hall Stone Jewel, which forms part of the Master's Craft regalia (see Rule 251, Book of Constitutions, and "Information for the Guidance of Members of the Craft") should not be worn by the Master at the dinner (or in the bar before dinner) if there are non-Masons present as waiters or bar staff, unless a dispensation has been given for the wearing of regalia at the after-proceedings. (A permanent dispensation exists within the Province of Buckinghamshire – the only Hall Stone Province – for the wearing of the jewel by the Masters of Buckinghamshire Lodges.)

The taking of wine ought to be kept within due bounds, but this is, of course, a matter in which the Master should be guided as to the practice in the individual Lodge by the Immediate Past Master or the Director of Ceremonies. As a matter of principle, however, it is better that the Master should not take wine with anyone who will be the subject of a toast after dinner, and also if he does not call on all the Brethren to take wine with an individual or class with whom he has himself just taken wine.

It is a matter of courtesy to ensure that wine-taking is confined to the intervals between courses.

Whether it is the Immediate Past Master or the Director of Ceremonies who takes charge of the taking of wine, the correct procedure is for the Master to gavel at the appropriate moment, for *only* the Master should use the Master's gavel. It is quite wrong for the Immediate Past Master to take the gavel at any time. It is the

Master who is presiding at dinner, and the gavel is the symbol of his authority there, just as it is in the Lodge.

After dinner, the Master should take care that he does not forget Grace before he proceeds to the toasts.

The first toast is "The Queen and the Craft", and if fire is to be given after the other toasts, it should be given after this also. Moreover, if the National Anthem is sung at this point, it must follow the proposal, but precede the drinking, of this toast (see the Report of the Board of General Purposes adopted by Grand Lodge in December, 1985). It is important that the Master sets an example to the rest of the Brethren by standing firmly to attention while the National Anthem is sung – a convention all too frequently ignored these days even by Brethren who are old enough to know better. In connection with the second and third toasts it should be noted that only the Grand Master has a second "The" in his title ("The Most Worshipful The Grand Master" but "The Most Worshipful Pro Grand Master"). Current practice in the case of this and the succeeding toasts is to give the Masonic office (or rank) and name of the individual who is the subject of the toast, but to omit orders and decorations (the so-called "honorifics"), even though they may be printed on the formal toast list.

After the first two toasts it is customary to give the Brethren permission to smoke, though once that stage has been reached in the after-proceedings the Brethren do not strictly require permission. Regard must also now be had to the requirements of Health and Safety legislation.

The third toast is a long one, and inexperienced Masters are sometimes apt to try break it down into what appear to be its constituent parts. The toast is, however, to *all* of the Pro (*not* Provincial) Grand Master, the Deputy Grand Master, the Assistant Grand Master and the rest of the Grand Officers present and past (*not* past and present). Rather too often, Brethren standing to drink this toast can be heard to murmur "Grand Lodge", but that is quite wrong. All present Wardens and Masters, together with subscribing

Past Masters, of Lodges are members of *Grand Lodge*, but they do not all fall within the scope of this toast, which is to *Grand Officers*.

Most of the remaining toasts call for no special comment, but the Master should note that the toast to Absent Brethren, although it has no fixed place in the list of toasts, but is frequently drunk at nine o'clock, must not precede the drinking of the loyal toast or that to the Grand Master (see "Information for the Guidance of Members of the Craft"). Finally, the Master gives a double knock, not preceded by a single one, to summon the Tyler (or whoever) to propose the Tyler's toast.

Chapter 16

The Installing Master

There are several good reasons for dealing with the duties of the Installing Master in a separate chapter. First, the ceremony of Installation is later in date than the other ceremonies, only reaching its modern form more than ten years after the three degree ceremonies had been settled. Secondly, the ceremony differs markedly in its basic structure from those of the three degrees, so that the approach of "compare and contrast" which I have adopted in the preceding chapters would be of little help. Thirdly, in most regular Lodges the Director of Ceremonies undertakes a significant part of the work which is carried out in Emulation Lodge of Improvement by the Installing Master; this potential separation of duties, which does not occur in any of the other ceremonies, is more easily dealt with in a chapter devoted to the Installation ceremony alone.

In Emulation Lodge of Improvement, the Installation ceremony is always worked in full, even though, as a matter of necessity, the Brother acting as Master Elect will invariably be an Installed Master. In a regular Lodge, however, if the Master Elect is already an Installed Master, there are certain adjustments which are habitually made with the aim of shortening the ceremony. These are not, strictly, Emulation working and the words suggested in the printed Ritual to meet this situation should not therefore be regarded as fixed and immutable. The customary adjustments are noted below at the relevant places.

Before the ceremony begins, the Master asks Entered Apprentices to retire, and then, if the Wardens' chairs are not already occupied by Installed Masters, he invites qualified Brethren to assume those positions. If, as is usually the case, the Senior Warden is the Master Elect he, at least, will have to be replaced. In a regular Lodge, the Inner Guard, if a Master Mason, will also normally be replaced at this point, although in Emulation Lodge of Improvement this last is sometimes deferred until the Master Masons retire for the Inner Working. It is this placing of Installed Masters into the Wardens' chairs which creates the Board of Installed Masters, which is formally constituted at a later part of the ceremony.

The Lodge is then opened or resumed in the second degree, and the Master Elect is presented to the Installing Master (and thereby the other two members of the Board of Installed Masters). In Emulation Lodge of Improvement, this presentation is made by the member of the Committee who is acting as Preceptor; in a regular Lodge it may be done by a Past Master, but is more commonly done by the Director of Ceremonies. In the former case, the Master replies to the presentation with the words "Brother Past Master ....., your presentation shall be attended to ..."; in the latter case, his reply is "Brother Director of Ceremonies, your presentation ..."

This is perhaps an appropriate point to mention that in a regular Lodge too slavish an adherence to the published wording of the Emulation Ritual in the ceremony of Installation is more likely to lead to the Brother in the Chair talking nonsense than in any other ceremony. When I write "nonsense" I am not referring to matters of controversy where there is scope for differences of opinion – every working, including Emulation, has adherents who are all too ready to characterise as nonsense ritual practices with which they do not agree: I mean clear and undoubted nonsense. It quite frequently happens that the outgoing Master does not install his successor. Sometimes the reason is that the outgoing Master is unable to be present; sometimes it is the established custom of the Lodge that a senior member of the Craft carries out the ceremony on his behalf. In either case it is nonsense for the Installing Master to state unblushingly "...that he may receive from his predecessor the benefit of Installation, the better to qualify him...". Better by far to follow the Grand Lodge practice of expanding the formula to "...that he may receive from his predecessor, *or some other duly qualified Brother*, the benefit of Installation, the better to qualify him..." There are other instances to which I shall draw attention elsewhere in this chapter.

A very common mistake in reciting the various qualifications for the Master's Chair is to omit from the third clause the word "and" before "steady and firm in principle", overlooking the fact that the words "able and willing etc." are in apposition to what has just gone before and not further and additional qualifications.

When the Master Elect is a Master Mason, the Secretary will read the Ancient Charges at the conclusion of the Installing Master's recital of the qualifications and afterwards the Master Elect will indicate his submission to them. If, however, the Master Elect is an Installed Master, instead of directing his attention to the Secretary for the Ancient Charges, the Installing Master uses a formula such as "At your installation on a previous occasion you signified your assent to those Ancient Charges and Regulations. Do you now confirm that assent?" (Or use the words at the end of the Inner Working supplied for use with the Emulation Ritual.) Whether or not the Master Elect is already an Installed Master, the Master directs him to advance to the pedestal and take a solemn obligation as regards his duties as Master of that Lodge. It is better if this direction is delivered without a pause, although as I have indicated in Chapter 14, the Master Elect may advance either after the word "pedestal" or at the end of the sentence. The Installing Master should ensure that the Master Elect has removed his glove before he places his hand on the V.S.L.. If the Master Elect is a Master Mason, he dictates the Obligation to him in the usual way (though he can generally use longer phrases than he would in the case of a Candidate for one of the three degrees); but if the Master Elect is an Installed Master, he usually leaves him to recite his Obligation unaided, using the formula "Repeat your name at length and recite the Obligation."

A common mistake in the early part of the Obligation is to get the phrasing wrong, something which is much more readily apparent when a previously installed Master Elect is reciting it rather than it being dictated by the Installing Master. All too often, it is phrased: "do agree to accept the office of Master of this Lodge and the duties thereof / faithfully, zealously and impartially to administer / to the best etc.". The correct division of the phrases is: "do agree to accept the office of Master of this Lodge / and the duties thereof faithfully, zealously and impartially to administer / to the best etc.".

After the Obligation has been sealed, the Installing Master raises the Master Elect, and if, as is the case in Emulation Lodge of Improvement, the Lodge has already been opened in the third degree and is then merely to be resumed, he may immediately ask Fellow Crafts to retire and then raise the Lodge, leaving the Master Elect standing before the pedestal. If, however, the Lodge has then to be opened in full in the third degree, he should wait for a moment while the Director of Ceremonies, or a Past Master, leads the Master Elect to a seat, preferably on the south side of the Lodge no more than a few places away from the Director of Ceremonies.

After the Lodge has been opened or resumed in the third degree, the Master asks Master Masons to retire. No fixed formula is provided in the Emulation Ritual, but it is the practice in Emulation Lodge of Improvement to use some such words as "I must now ask all below the rank of Installed Master to retire from the Lodge for a short time" (*not* "the rank of *an* Installed Master").

When the Master Masons have left the Lodge, the Inner Guard closes and locks the door. Meanwhile in Emulation Lodge of Improvement two members of the precepting Committee pick up the kneeling stool at the Master's pedestal by either end and with it drive the Master Elect backwards some four or five paces; they lower the stool to the ground, the one on the right of the Master Elect gives him a whispered instruction to kneel and show the sign of R. at the words "Let us pray", and they both sit. In a regular Lodge, the placing of the kneeling stool will normally be done by the Director of Ceremonies and the Assistant Director of Ceremonies. If the Lodge has merely been resumed in the third degree, with the Master Elect standing before the pedestal, they can follow the Emulation practice, but if the Lodge has been opened in full, they will generally position the kneeling stool before the Director of Ceremonies collects the Master Elect and leads him to it. If the Master Elect is not already an Installed Master, he will probably not appreciate that he has to kneel for the prayer as well as give the sign of R., and it is therefore most important that the Director of Ceremonies gives him a whispered instruction to that effect.

Only when the Master Elect has taken up his position in front of the kneeling stool does the Installing Master constitute the Board of Installed Masters. In addition, the Installing Master should note that this is one of the very few occasions when the Master does not gavel before changing the status of the Lodge; he gavels only *after* he has declared the Board constituted.

In Emulation Lodge of Improvement, the Installing Master delivers the prayer; in most Lodges in which a Chaplain is appointed that Officer will deliver it. At the conclusion of the prayer, the Installing Master waits for the kneeling stool to be replaced in front of the Master's pedestal, before he proceeds with the ceremony. As in the case of the Obligation of the Master Elect in the second degree he must ensure that the latter has removed his gloves before he places his hands on the V.S.L. for the Obligation. Even though the Brethren are already standing, he must not forget to gavel before he dictates the Obligation, or that it is the p...l sign of the third degree which is held throughout the Obligation.

There are conflicting views as to the correct procedure to be followed at this point if the Master Elect is already an Installed Master. It is generally agreed that he should not take the Obligation again, and it is also certain that he must be kneeling with his right hand readily accessible so that he can be raised at the appropriate point. The Emulation Ritual (which in this particular situation, as has been explained above, cannot reflect the actual practice in Emulation Lodge of Improvement) suggests that the Master Elect be directed to kneel, place both hands on the V.S.L., and re-affirm his Obligation by sealing it etc.. Many, however, take the view – I am one of them – that even to seal the Obligation again is unnecessary and inappropriate, and that it is better if the Master Elect does not even place his hands on the V.S.L. at this point. It is sufficient if he is directed to advance to the pedestal, kneel and place both hands on the pedestal to either side of the V.S.L.. I must stress, however, that this is entirely a matter of personal preference, and that an Installing Master should be ready to be guided as to the established practice in his individual Lodge.

After the sealing of the Obligation (if appropriate), the Installing Master explains to a Master Mason the penalty (but does not, of course, do so to an Installed Master). It should be noted here that the meaning of "s...g over" is "left hanging from". In both cases, however, he does explain the three great lights before proceeding to raise the Master Elect. This latter action is one that is frequently performed incorrectly. The Installing Master leaves his pedestal by the south side and stands close to the side of it facing west, roughly level with the front of the pedestal. He takes the Master Elect's r.w. between the t. and ff. of his own r.h., leans across to place his l.h. above the other's l.b., fairly close to the s......r, and as he says "Rise, ..." presses backwards with his l.h. forcing the Master Elect to stand and wheel backwards through ninety degrees so that he is facing north. He places the Master Elect a pace or so in front of the position usually occupied by the Director of Ceremonies, and himself takes up a position on, or a little to the north of, the centre-line of the Lodge, facing south; i.e. so that they are standing respectively in very roughly the positions occupied by the Candidate and the Master for the communication of the secrets in the third degree.

He then proceeds to communicate the secrets of an Installed Master. The first of the signs is given with the head turned to the right, and the movements with the right arm may be given with the hand open or with the first and second fingers extended side by side and the remaining fingers held to the palm with the thumb. In either case, however, the right hand touches the right shoulder at each movement, and after the final movement is dropped direct to the side. The g..p is given by the Installing Master advancing, and taking the other's r.w. between his own r. t. and ff. on the word "thus", placing his open left hand under the Master Elect's right forearm a little above the wrist on the word "saying", and sliding it up to the elbow as he completes the sentence; then replacing the other's hand at his side. He steps back to his former position as he explains the signification of the word.

The final sign is given with the r.h., from l. s......r to a point outside the right leg, whilst stepping back with the r.f. and bowing slightly. I must emphasise that arm and r.f. move simultaneously; it is wrong for the sign to be given in two distinct movements. Finally the r.f. is brought back to a position side by side with the l.f., keeping the r.h. beside the leg; there should be no "recovery" with the hand to the s......r, however commonly it may be seen done that way. This sign, indeed, is to be seen given in many – and wondrous – ways which are not in accordance with Emulation working. It is properly given in a simple fashion without ostentation. There should be no flourish with the right hand, nor any profound bow; trying to touch the ground with the forehead, which is sometimes to be observed, produces a somewhat unedifying posture.

The Installing Master then again advances to the Master Elect and divests him of his Master Mason's badge before investing him with that of an Installed Master. Only when he has done so should he say the words "I now invest you ....", holding the corner of the badge with his left hand as does the Senior Warden in the three degrees. He releases it after a moment in order to invest him with the jewel. He takes the latter in his left hand at the words "The Sq. being" and releases it again either after "virtue" or after "actions"; either is in accordance with Emulation working.

If, however, the Master Elect is already an Installed Master, then immediately after raising him and placing him in the position already mentioned the Installing Master will adopt a formula such as "You are already in possession of the secrets of an Installed Master, and you wear the badge of that rank. I now invest you with the jewel of your office, which is the highest ..." The remainder of the Inner Working follows the same course as if the Master Elect is a Master Mason.

The Installing Master takes the Master Elect's r.w. by the g..p, places his l.h. on the other's l. s......r and whispers to him to do likewise and to step off with the left foot. Then he steps backwards with his right foot and, passing from north to south between the pedestal and the Chair, positions the Master Elect in front of the latter. Only then does he say, "With the g. ...", pressing the Master Elect *gently* into the Chair at the word "place". If there is sufficient room, he may give the sign of H. from where he stands; otherwise, he may step back a pace or two (no more) before giving it (remember: arm and r.f. move together). He should not move on to the floor of the Lodge to give the sign – indeed, if there is a dais in the east, he should not move off the dais at this point.

After he has presented the gavel to the Master Elect, he should wait for the latter to replace it on the pedestal before directing him to invest the Immediate Past Master; a whispered or mouthed instruction may be helpful here (rather as when the Master instructs the Candidate in the sign(s) in any of the three degrees). If the Immediate Past Master is absent, not only must this small part of the ceremony be omitted, but also the Immediate Past Master may not be invested on any future occasion (see "Information for the Guidance of Members of the Craft").

The Installing Master then turns to face west and calls on the Brethren to salute the new Master. It is important that he observes the correct sequence of words and actions at this point. After the words "time from me", he turns to face the Master, says "To order, Brethren", takes a step and then gives the G. or R. sign five times.

(In some other workings it is the sign of Hy. that is given here, and indeed that is the current practice of the Rulers of the Craft when one of them installs the new Master of a Lodge.) The Installing Master should particularly note that the Emulation formula at this point, and during the proclamation that follows each of the perambulations, is "taking *the* time *from* me", and not "taking your time with me". Finally, he turns again to face west, and standing close by the left-hand side of the pedestal closes the Board, leaning across the pedestal at the end of the formula in order to gavel. (Again, some very senior Brethren prefer the new Master to gavel at this point, making the point that it is he who is now in the Chair.) After the Wardens have repeated his knock, he waits for the other Brethren to sit, before, still standing in the same position, he directs the Inner Guard to admit Master Masons.

As the Master Masons re-enter the Lodge, the Installing Master takes up a position at the east end of the line formed in the north, facing south and about two paces from the eastern edge of the carpet. When the line is complete he gives the direction, then turns left, and leads off the line, taking a pace or two before squaring the Lodge at the north-east corner. He halts with his feet in the step in front of the Master's pedestal and salutes to the point of recovery, facing to the front throughout. There is no need to halt and *then* take a step when saluting during this or the succeeding perambulations. He leads the line round the Lodge back to the starting point, squaring at each corner, and turns again to face south. He will need to maintain a relatively sedate pace during the early part of the perambulation because each Brother behind him halts at the Master's pedestal and therefore if he is not careful the line of Brethren will become widely strung out; once all the Brethren have passed the pedestal he can afford to increase the pace a little. (In some workings, the Lodge is not squared and the salute is given in passing. That is the course adopted when one of the Rulers carries out the ceremony.) Leaving the Master Masons in line, he makes his way to the south side of the Master's pedestal for the first proclamation, at the conclusion of which he leads the salutes to the Master. It is again important that he observes the correct sequence of words and actions at this point. After the words "time from me", he turns to face the Master, says "To order, Brethren", takes a step and then gives the G. or R. sign three times.

Another instance of the nonsense to which I referred earlier arises if a Lodge – typically an Installed Masters' Lodge – has no Master Masons among its members. It has in recent years become the almost universal practice not to include visiting Master Masons in the perambulations, either from a mistaken belief that the duties of hospitality render it discourteous to ask visitors to join in the salutes (though no such scruples extend to the Inner Working) or from a – perhaps well-founded – suspicion that they may not be equal to the task. Now, there may be very good practical reasons in Lodges with no shortage of members for visiting Master Masons being asked to resume their seats and confining the salutes to the members of the Lodge, but such a practice has unfortunately become the norm. However, if the Lodge insists on making up its "saluting party" from its own members, all of whom are Installed Masters, the Installing Master should at least tailor the proclamations to suit the circumstances: "Brethren, during the temporary absence of certain Brethren, Brother ...... has been etc." is sensible; the normal formula "Brethren, during your temporary absence, Brother ...... has been etc." is not. And if there are no Master Masons at all present, it is not counter to the spirit of Emulation working to say: "Brethren, Brother ...... has been etc.".

If, as is generally the case, the Lodge's practice is for the Director of Ceremonies to lead the perambulations and salutes, the Installing Master does not move from his position at the south of the pedestal after he has directed the Inner Guard to admit the Master Masons, but gives the direction to pass round the Lodge from that position, and then waits until the line is re-formed in the north before proceeding with the proclamation. The Director of Ceremonies meanwhile leads the procession round in exactly the same way as the

Installing Master would have done, and remains in the north facing south while the proclamation is made. In this case, the proclamation ends with the words "time from the Director of Ceremonies". The Installing Master stands fast, and the Director of Ceremonies walks due south to a position immediately in front of the first row of seats, parks his wand, turns to face the Master, says "To order, Brethren" and leads the salutes. (The Installing Master does not turn or salute.) The Director of Ceremonies then takes up his wand again and returns to his former position at the east end of the line in the north.

The Installing Master then presents the W.Ts., which should have been placed in readiness for him by the outgoing Immediate Past Master. If the third degree has already been worked in the course of the meeting, it is not necessary for the full explanation to be given, and the Installing Master, having named the W.Ts. – this is essential – adds words such as "Their uses and significations have already been explained this evening, so I will not detain you with a repetition." This formula is not one which is fixed, and slight variations in wording are therefore permissible. In many regular Lodges, if the Master Elect is already an Installed Master, a similar procedure is adopted, using words such as "Their uses and significations are already well known to you, so I will not detain you by explaining them at length."

The Installing Master then directs the Master to close the Lodge in the third degree, and immediately sits. In Emulation Lodge of Improvement he occupies the chair at the east end of the front row on the south side, but in a regular Lodge he will normally occupy the Immediate Past Master's seat. After the Lodge has been closed in the third degree (or, as is more usual in a regular Lodge, resumed in the second), he stands once again immediately to the left of the Master's pedestal and directs the Inner Guard to admit Fellow Crafts. He then makes his way to the head of the line and proceeds as in the third degree. Alternatively, if the Director of Ceremonies leads the perambulations, the Installing Master stands fast until the last of the Brethren has passed him, and then joins the end of the line. In either case, when he reaches the north side of the Senior Warden's pedestal he wheels left, and stands immediately to the left of the pedestal, where he waits until the line has re-formed in the north before making the proclamation. The procedure is similar to that in the third degree, but as the Installing Master is already facing the new Master he does not need to turn before he calls the Brethren to order if he leads the salutes. He takes the step and sign which he holds, and says "B., h., b.." in the correct rhythm of the salute (as in the knocks of the degree), but does not suit the action to the words, which are merely the method of conveying the time to the Brethren. He *then* gives the salute to the same rhythm. The same procedure is followed by the Director of Ceremonies if it is he who leads the salutes, though he does so from the south-east part of the Lodge as in the third degree. It is very noticeable that there is a strong tendency, particularly among the Brethren in the line, to even out the intervals between the individual elements of the salute so that the rhythm becomes that of the first degree knocks; for that reason it is as well if the Installing Master or the Director of Ceremonies exaggerates slightly the uneven rhythm.

After the salute, the Installing Master makes his way without squaring direct to the south side of the Master's pedestal and there presents the W.Ts. as in the third degree, before directing the Master to close the Lodge in the second degree.

That done, standing once more immediately to the left of the Master's pedestal, he directs the Inner Guard to admit Entered Apprentices. He proceeds exactly as in the second degree, except that this time he wheels left at the west of the Junior Warden's pedestal, taking up a position immediately to the left of it for the proclamation. If he leads the salutes, he may either turn to face the Master before calling the Brethren to order, or he may instead remain facing north for the salutes and turn only his head.

After the W.Ts. have been presented, the Installing Master directs the Brethren to sit. Once they have done so, he presents the Warrant to the new Master (who in Emulation working does not stand to receive it). When the Master returns it to him, he should pass it to the outgoing Immediate Past Master to fold and put away in its case. The Book of Constitutions and the By-laws are then presented. Since 1979 a shortened formula for the presentation of the latter is permissible and, indeed, seems now to be becoming the norm. For those working at Emulation Lodge of Improvement I should add that either version may be used on a Friday evening, but no mercy will be shown to an Installing Master who elects to use the older – and longer – formula and fails to get it right!

If the Lodge has a Hall Stone Jewel, it is transferred to the new Master at this point. There is no official form of wording prescribed, but the Appendix to the Emulation Ritual contains a formula to cover the situation. I should, however, stress that none of the material in the Appendix to the Ritual is a part of Emulation working – at any rate in the context in which it appears there. (The explanation of the first degree Tracing Board in the Appendix is largely composed of parts of the First Lecture "stitched together", and the so-called long explanation of the second degree W.Ts. is actually the explanation of the movable jewels from the Fifth Section of the First Lecture.)

After directing the Master to appoint and invest his Officers, the Installing Master (or the Director of Ceremonies) moves straight to a point on the mid-line of the Lodge some five or six paces from the Master's pedestal. With step and sign, he asks, "Worshipful Master, whom do you appoint your Senior Warden?" On receiving the reply, he discharges the sign and makes his way to the Senior Warden's pedestal where he collects the collar and jewel, gavel and column. He then makes his way to the Brother named, who will have stood as soon as his name was announced by the Master, and conducts him to the north or south side of the pedestal, as appropriate. He hands the collar to the Master and should assist him by pinning the Officer's collar under the collar of his jacket or coat. He hands the other items to the Master as required and at the end conducts the Senior Warden to his place. In Emulation working the Installing Master does not give a court bow to the newly invested Officer, or at any point in the ceremony. He then conducts the Brother who acted as Senior Warden of the Board of Installed Masters to a vacant seat and makes his way back to the point on the mid-line of the Lodge, where he repeats the procedure for the Junior Warden and the other Officers. It should be noted that the Wardens are the Master's (so "... appoint *your* Senior/Junior Warden") whereas the other Officers are the Lodge's (so, e.g., "... appoint Secretary").

In Emulation Lodge of Improvement the Treasurer, as a very senior member of the Craft, rarely attends meetings, so that the formula used is: "Worshipful Master, the Treasurer is absent. Whom do you appoint Secretary?" On those occasions when the Treasurer is present, the Installing Master invites the Master to invest him, though no precise words are laid down for him to use. In a regular Lodge, the Director of Ceremonies will normally invite the Worshipful Master to invest the Brother who has been elected Tyler and conduct him to and from the pedestal, though if the Lodge has exercised its power under Rule 113 to allow the Master to appoint a subscribing member to the office (without emolument), he will use the same formula as for the other Officers. In Emulation Lodge of Improvement the procedure is different. The Installing Master, when he has conducted the Inner Guard to his place and accommodated the Brother who had charge of the door during the ceremony with a seat, himself occupies a chair at the west end of the front row of seats in the north. When the Master summons the Tyler with the double knock, the Inner Guard admits the Tyler, who makes his way unescorted to the edge of the carpet, carrying the sword by the hilt, point downwards, in his left hand and with his collar draped over his left arm, salutes and makes his own way to the Master's pedestal to be invested. When the Tyler has resumed his place outside the door, the Installing Master stands, moves to the north side of the Senior Warden's pedestal and continues with the ceremony.

In Emulation Lodge of Improvement the Installing Master delivers all three addresses; the first from the left of the Senior Warden and the other two from the left of the Master. They call for no comment beyond the observation that the address to the Master contains one of the three instances of the word "upon" in Emulation working.

I have already dealt with the modifications to the ceremony when the Master Elect is a Past Master. It happens, however, from time to time that the Master continues in office for a second year, either because he has been re-elected or because some mishap affecting the Brother elected to serve as Master has brought into play Rule 107 or 108 of the Book of Constitutions. Brethren are often at a loss as to the procedure to be followed on such an occasion, and indeed there is no one correct way of dealing with the situation. It is, however, utterly wrong for an incumbent Master to be reinstalled: at his own installation he will have been obligated and proclaimed as Master until the next regular period of election within the Lodge *and* until a successor shall have been duly elected *and* installed in his stead. There is a note available from the Grand Secretary's Office, headed "NOT OFFICIAL" which gives a suggested procedure to meet the situation, but there are other ways of proceeding. The suggestions I make below are based on, but are not exactly the same as, those in the note.

The summons for the Installation Meeting will normally, if the Master has been elected to continue for a second year, include an item such as "To proclaim the Worshipful Master" or "To proclaim W Bro. .... as Master", but merely "To invest the Officers" would not be wrong. If the outgoing Master is continuing because of the provisions of Rule 107 or 108, then the summons will show the normal item "To install the Master Elect." It is unnecessary to place Installed Masters in the Wardens' chairs, since there is no Board of Installed Masters on such an occasion; similarly, it is unnecessary to replace the Inner Guard temporarily. Some Lodges may, however, prefer to do both, either because it is perceived as giving a greater degree of formality to the proceedings or because of a reluctance, as mentioned in Chapter 11, to leave a Warden's chair temporarily vacant.

As a bare minimum it is sufficient, with the Lodge still in the first degree, for the Immediate Past Master or the Director of Ceremonies to move straight to a point on the mid-line of the Lodge a few paces from the Master's pedestal and with step and sign ask, "Worshipful Master, you having been re-elected as Master of this Lodge (or Worshipful Master, the Master Elect having been prevented by .... from undertaking the Office of Master of this Lodge), whom do you appoint your Senior Warden?" The investiture of the Officers then proceeds as normal. It is clearly unnecessary to deliver the address to the Master, but if either of the Wardens has changed since the previous year the address to the Wardens and the address to the Brethren should be delivered; the latter address is directed to all except the Master and Wardens and so, strictly, should not be delivered if neither Warden has changed, but Lodges may wish to deliver it nevertheless to round off the ceremony.

If the reason for the Master continuing in office for a second year is the death of the Master Elect (particularly as for Rule 107 to apply the death must have occurred less than seven days before the Installation meeting), a Lodge may feel that anything more elaborate than the minimum is inappropriate to the circumstances. In other cases, however, a Lodge may wish to adopt a slightly more elaborate procedure. There is no need for the Lodge to be opened beyond the first degree but, again, a Lodge may wish to go up into the third degree to give greater formality to the occasion. If, however, the Lodge is opened into the third degree, it is effectively committed to adopting in the second and first degree whatever procedure it follows in the third.

As there would otherwise have been no point in opening into the third degree, that procedure will inevitably include the proclamation of the Master, probably, though not necessarily, accompanied by a salute by way of greeting and possibly also preceded by the Master Masons passing round the Lodge and saluting him first. A possible form of proclamation is: "Brethren, Brother ...... having duly served for a full year as Master of the .... Lodge, No. .... on the Register of the Grand Lodge of England, has been re-elected to that office until the next regular period of election within this Lodge, and until a successor shall have been duly elected and installed in his stead." There are, however, various other forms of wording equally permissible – and various other permutations of the accompanying procedure.

There is no obvious reason why the W.Ts. should be presented again, but if they are it is better that they should not be explained in full. It is certainly wrong for the Warrant to be presented again to the Master, as it has never left his keeping, and the same applies to the Book of Constitutions, the By-laws and the Hall Stone Jewel (if any). Finally, the Master must not be presented with a Past Master's jewel, as he is not a Past Master until his successor has been installed; the fact that he served for two consecutive years may, however, properly be recorded on a bar to the jewel.

Chapter 17

The Immediate Past Master

Many Brethren as they install their successors in the chair heave a sigh of relief and sit back, intending if not to enjoy themselves, at least to relax a little. Such an attitude could hardly be more mistaken. If the Master has a difficult job in ruling the Lodge and conducting, or at least presiding over, its ceremonies, the Immediate Past Master has an even more demanding one; for he has to watch over his successor, to advise him, guide him and even, if possible, anticipate his every wrong move in the course of a Meeting.

The Immediate Past Master, if he performs his duties conscientiously, has, in fact, the most difficult job in the Lodge: for in performing the duties which I have listed above the Immediate Past Master must, above all things, exercise discretion. He must know when to act to correct, and when to leave well alone – the latter being by far the more important.

The Immediate Past Master must, therefore, be as familiar with the ritual as he was during his own year as Master, and he must be even more wide-awake, so that he may spot any error as – if not before – it happens. To be able to do this, there is no substitute for having the work off by heart; the Immediate Past Master who has his nose buried in his Ritual Book (an object which is not allowed to be opened in Emulation Lodge of Improvement) is rarely able to act with the necessary promptness, simply because he is too immersed in the written word, and may even be reading a paragraph or two ahead when something goes wrong which he is too busy to see! But not only must he be able to recognise a mistake when it happens, he must also exercise an almost instantaneous judgement as to whether it is serious enough to be corrected, or whether (which is usually the case) it is relatively trivial and is much better left alone. The Immediate Past Master suffers from another disadvantage: when he was Master, and had been carefully preparing for the ceremonies, he will have had a good idea of those places in the ceremony where it was most likely that he would go astray, and could be on his guard as he approached the danger zone accordingly. As Immediate Past Master, unless he and the Master attend the same Lodge of Instruction or rehearse together regularly, he will have little idea where his services are most likely to be called upon.

Finally, the Immediate Past Master must understand that he is a *prompter* and *not* a preceptor. In a Lodge of Instruction, where the aim is to train Brethren to achieve the highest standards of work, every error should be corrected immediately. In a regular Lodge such an approach is disastrous – but is too often to be found. If the Immediate Past Master insists on correcting each small error, or allows the Master no pause to remember what comes next before he leaps in with a prompt, he will either demoralise the Master so that he becomes increasingly prone to make mistakes, or he will spoil the flow of the ceremony for the Candidate (who, it should not be forgotten, is the principal *raison d'être* of the whole proceeding); often, indeed, he will end up doing both.

In the openings and closings and the ceremonies themselves, the Immediate Past Master has little to say, and not a great deal more to do, apart from his supervising rôle already referred to, the importance of which cannot be overemphasised. In the course of opening the Lodge, in Emulation Lodge of Improvement he has the duty of responding with "So mote it be" at the end of the prayer; in most regular Lodges those words are spoken or sung by all the Brethren. In Emulation Lodge of Improvement, unlike many regular Lodges, he does not answer the question "The Master's place?" He does, however, open the V.S.L. and adjust the Sq. and Cs.. In Emulation Lodge of Improvement, this is done from his position to the left of the Master, and he does not move to the front of the pedestal to perform this function, still less give a court bow or salute when he has done it. Both of the latter are very commonly to be seen in regular Lodges; both are unnecessary, though of the two the former is probably preferable.

A word is desirable as to the positioning of the Sq. and Cs.: they should always be placed on the right-hand page, as viewed by the Master, because the Candidate's hand will be laid upon the other page in the first two degrees. (In Emulation working the V.S.L. is always orientated so that the Master can read it, with the angle of the Sq. and points of the Cs. towards the bottom of the page. Even in those workings where the bible is turned the other way, the Sq. and Cs. should always point towards the bottom of the page.) In the second degree, the procedure is straightforward, but it is worth noting that it is immaterial which of the two points of the Cs. is uncovered. It is also immaterial where the bible is opened; in Emulation working there are no significant passages varying according to the degree in which the Lodge is open. The only requirement is the common-sense one that the book should be opened somewhere near the middle so that the pages are roughly equal on each side and the Sq. and Cs. will therefore not slide about.

In the third degree opening the Immediate Past Master should not forget to take a step after adjusting the Sq. and Cs. in readiness for "All glory to the Most High".

No special problem occurs in any of the closings, but the newly invested Immediate Past Master should not forget that he has the final line to deliver at the very end of the closing. (See also Chapter 3 on the subject of the gesture that accompanies "F., F., F.".) It should be noted that Emulation working prescribes no position for the Sq. and Cs. after the V.S.L. has been closed; they may be placed on either the V.S.L. or the cushion on which it rests, and in as haphazard an arrangement as the Immediate Past Master wishes; it is essential only to break the orderly arrangement of the three great lights that obtains while the Lodge is open.

If the Lodge is called off, it is the Immediate Past Master's duty after the Master has given his single knock to close the V.S.L., leaving the Sq. and Cs. in position between the closed pages. In practice a prudent Immediate Past Master will slide the Sq. and Cs. carefully down the page, so that the angle of Sq. slightly protrudes from between the closed leaves; this will make it easier for him to reopen the V.S.L. when the Lodge is called back on.

During the ceremony of Initiation, and the other two degrees, the Immediate Past Master has to say "So mote it be" at the end of the prayer and to set out and clear away the W.Ts. at the appropriate points in the ceremony. In Emulation, unlike some other workings, the W.Ts. are not put out as the Lodge is opened in each degree, but only when they are required for presentation to the Candidate or the newly installed Master. In the first two degrees the W.Ts. should be laid out as soon as the Candidate has left the Master's pedestal after being entrusted with the secrets, and cleared away after he retires to restore his comfort. In the third degree, they should be laid out after the Candidate retires to restore his comfort, and cleared at the conclusion of the ceremony.

In the first degree, the Immediate Past Master must be ready to hand the Master the Warrant, and then the Book of Constitutions and By-Laws together, at the appropriate moment, receiving back and, if necessary, folding the Warrant in due course. In the second degree he passes the Sq. to the Senior Deacon at the appropriate moment just before the Obligation. During the Traditional History in the third degree, the Immediate Past Master hands the Master the small Tracing Board at the appropriate moment, together with the pencil from the W.Ts., which he will have previously laid out. In the ceremony of Installation, he performs a similar function with the Warrant, Book of Constitutions and the By-Laws for the Installing Master, and it is essential that he lays out the W.Ts. also, since the Installing Master is otherwise engaged. Towards the end of the Inner Working he hands the Immediate Past Master's collar to the Installing Master so that the new Master may invest the former with it, but despite this formal handover, he, like the Installing Master, still has some residual functions to carry out during the remainder of the ceremony.

In Emulation Lodge of Improvement, the member of the Committee acting as Immediate Past Master also carries out the duties of Preceptor (or perhaps I should put it the other way round, as on a Friday evening precepting is his primary function). It is he, rather than the Master, who asks the questions in the Lectures, if worked, and who inspects the ballot box both before and after the ballot has taken place – a proceeding which would be unusual, though not actually wrong, in a regular Lodge.

In many Lodges the Immediate Past Master will be in charge of the taking of wine at dinner. It will therefore be prudent for him to familiarise himself with the section on the After-Proceedings in Chapter 21.

Chapter 18

The Lectures

It is not the purpose of this chapter to go into detail on the history of the Lectures; to explain how they were originally the method by which most of the instruction of Freemasonry was carried out; how Emulation used the Grand Stewards' Lodge system of working the Lectures, and continued to do so when The Grand Stewards' Lodge ceased to give public demonstrations of them at twice-yearly Public Nights after 1867, so that they have now come to be called the Emulation Lectures.

Nonetheless it is the case that Emulation did adopt the Grand Stewards' system, and that today at the Annual Festival at the end of February the Deacons and Inner Guard of The Grand Stewards' Lodge occupy those offices to perpetuate the long-standing link.

It will be sufficient to recall that in its earliest days Emulation Lodge of Improvement used the Lectures as the means of teaching the ceremonies, and it was only some time in the 1830s that it began to rehearse the ceremonies themselves.

There is one Lecture for each of the three degrees, cast in catechetical form (that is, question and answer), and each contains a description of the ceremony of the degree to which it relates, and some additional material. The First Lecture consists of seven sections – five long and two short – of which the second and third describe the ceremony of Initiation adding some comment upon it, while the remainder are given up to descriptions of various Masonic virtues and characteristics, interspersed with biblical stories. Similarly, the second lecture consists of five sections, the greater part of which are given up to a description of the ceremony and the

Tracing Board, but which nonetheless incorporate an explanation of the origin and purpose of Geometry, a description of the six periods of the Creation, and full explanations of the five noble Orders of Architecture and the seven Liberal Arts and Sciences. The third lecture has only three sections, and consequently there is room for very little additional material – essentially only a full explanation of the f. ps. o. f..

Although the Lectures are worked far less frequently today than in former times, they do repay study, since they contain many passages of beautiful ritual, most of which will not have acquired that air of familiarity which leads to a jaded palate. They are worked through regularly at Emulation Lodge of Improvement twice in the course of the year, during the second half of its meetings. It is perhaps not generally realised that the test questions before Passing and Raising are taken from the First and Second Lectures respectively, and that when the Master offers to put others if any Brother wishes him to do so, any other question from the respective Lecture may be put by any member of the Lodge.

A Lodge which finds itself without a Candidate is afforded a useful opportunity to make use of the Lectures, either as a means of rehearsing the ceremonies (their original purpose), or to broaden the Masonic horizons of its members. Such a Lodge may either import members of Emulation Lodge of Improvement to demonstrate one or two Lecture sections (the Secretary is always glad to arrange for a "team" to visit a Lodge, provided that not too much travel is involved), or may show greater enterprise by parcelling out the work among its own members, probably in relatively short "bites" to reduce the burden of learning.

In Emulation Lodge of Improvement, the Lectures are worked (that is, the questions are put) by the member of the Committee acting as Preceptor (except at the Annual Festival in February, when they are worked from the Chair by the member of the Committee acting as Master), assisted by the Senior Warden (who gives the answers). If for some reason the Senior Warden is unable or unwilling to assist (increasingly common these days), the Junior Warden or another Brother will act as a substitute. The Wardens when assisting do so from their pedestals; other Brethren stand to the right of the Senior Warden immediately in front of the Inner Guard.

In Emulation Lodge of Improvement, as it is a Master Masons' Lodge, the Lectures are normally worked with the Lodge open in the third degree. In a regular Lodge, however, they may be worked in any degree which is at least as high as that to which the Lecture relates. Each section is introduced by the Master with the formula "Brother Senior Warden," – the Senior Warden stands in his place – "Will you assist Brother Past Master ... [or me] to work the ... section of the ... Lecture?" The Senior Warden replies "I will do my best, Worshipful Master." He then takes a step and gives the sign of the degree in which the Lodge is then open (*not* the sign of the degree of which the Lecture is about to be worked). If the Lecture is worked with the assistance of the Junior Warden, the same procedure is adopted; but if with the assistance of another Officer or Brother, the assistant is addressed by office or name, as the case may be, and makes the same reply, but does not salute until he has taken up his position in front of the Inner Guard.

When all the questions have been put and answered, the Brother working the section introduces the Charge with the appropriate formula, and leads the fire which accompanies it. This is in most cases identical to the greeting given to the newly installed Master in the appropriate degree at his Installation, but with everyone seated except the Brother who has been assisting. At the conclusion of the final section of each of the first two Lectures, however, when all the Brethren will have been brought to their feet a few moments before, full fire is given, identical to that given after each Masonic toast at dinner, but at a sedate pace so that the sign can be given in its proper place. Finally, the Lecture Master says "Thank you, Brother Senior Warden [or as appropriate]". The assistant then salutes again and resumes his seat.

The following points relate to the individual Lecture sections.

First Lecture, Section 1:

There are no obvious traps. At the appropriate point the Brother assisting salutes the Master with step and sign.

First Lecture, Section 2:

This section is difficult more because of its length than for any other reason – there are sixty-four questions and answers to be delivered. All stand with the appropriate sign when the Master and Wardens gavel for the prayer and the Obligation, and sit again immediately after.

First Lecture, Section 3:

At the appropriate points the Brother assisting salutes the Master with step and sign.

   If the Senior Warden assists in working this section, it is customary to communicate the Tn. to either the Junior Deacon or the Inner Guard; but any other Brother assisting will communicate it to the Senior Warden. In either case both Brethren must take a step first. The Officer confirming the correctness of the Tn. salutes the Master with step and the sign of the degree in which the Lodge is then open. (This is an exception to the principle mentioned in Chapter 3, that a Brother does not stand to order when an exchange is initiated by an Officer senior to him. Further examples are to be found in the Fifth Section of this Lecture and the First Section of the Second.)

First Lecture, Section 4:

At the appropriate point the Brother assisting shows the Sn. of R.

128   *Emulation Working Today*

First Lecture, Section 5:

The Master and Wardens have one answer each to deliver in the course of this section. The Master remains seated to deliver his, and holds up the jewel on the end of his collar with his left hand. Each Warden stands when addressed and, maintaining step and sign, holds up the jewel on the end of his collar with his left hand while he speaks. The Junior Warden, however, discharges the sign, releases his jewel and sits before he delivers the final part of his answer; this procedure has considerable similarity with that when the newly installed Master invests the Junior Warden during the Installation ceremony.

First Lecture, Section 6:

During the explanation of the four original forms in Freemasonry and of the four cardinal virtues, no step is taken when the E.A. sign is given; this, presumably, because it is not a salute to the Master, but constitutes a reference to a part of the body. For a similar reason, the position of the thumb is immaterial in the next gesture. The remaining two movements are, it is to be hoped, self-explanatory.

First Lecture, Section 7:

The Brother assisting in this section salutes the Master and each Warden with step and sign at the appropriate point; if either Warden assists he salutes the remaining two out of the three. All the Brethren are brought to their feet towards the end of the final answer, so that they are standing when the fire is given.

Second Lecture, Section 1:

A straightforward "ritual" section, with no special complications. All stand with the appropriate sign when the Master and Wardens gavel for the prayer and the Obligation. The same procedure is observed for communicating the Tn. as in the Third Section of the First Lecture.

Second Lecture, Section 2:

A beautiful, entirely "non-ritual" section, which deserves careful preparation on that account.

Second Lecture, Section 3:

This is essentially the first part of the Explanation of the second degree Tracing Board rendered into catechetical form. There is a slight trap in the answer to the question "Where were they ordered to be placed?" Because of a difference in the wording from that used in the Explanation of the Tracing Board, momentary inattention can lead to the greater part of the answer being omitted. The procedure for communicating the password is the same as for the Tn. in the First Section of the Lecture, except that neither Brother takes a step first.

Second Lecture, Section 4:

This, more than any other, is the section for adepts only. It is long, the explanations of some of the Orders of Architecture are sufficiently similar to provide a risk of their being muddled, and it requires considerable concentration to ensure that it is accurately rendered and put over in a fashion that will retain the attention of those listening.

Second Lecture, Section 5:

All the Brethren are brought to their feet towards the end of the Lecture, so that they are standing for the sign (which must not be given before the Word) and when the fire is given.

Third Lecture, Section 1:

A long, but fairly straightforward "ritual" section. All stand with the appropriate sign when the Master and Wardens gavel for the prayer and the Obligation. The procedure for giving two signs in succession at one point is similar to that employed in opening the Lodge in the third degree.

Third Lecture, Section 2:

A straightforward "ritual" section, comprising most of the Traditional History.

Third Lecture, Section 3:

There is nothing particularly to note in this section.

Chapter 19

Emulation Procedures

The purpose of this chapter is to describe, for the benefit of Brethren aspiring to work at Emulation Lodge of Improvement, and perhaps to gain a silver matchbox, the procedure which is followed each Friday evening, in working agreeably to the recognised system of Emulation Lodge of Improvement.

The work each Friday is divided into two parts, with a different member of the Committee acting as Preceptor for each part. In the first half of the evening one of the three degree ceremonies or the Installation is rehearsed, in rotation, after which the Lodge is called off. During the second half, a Lecture section is worked. (For the sake of historical completeness, until the end of 1997 in the first half of the evening one of the three degree ceremonies was rehearsed, in rotation; in the second half, the ceremony of Installation was worked on the first Friday in October and the third and fifth Fridays of every month, while on the remaining Fridays one long or two short Lecture sections were worked. The old practice is retained on the first Friday in October, when the Master's work is demonstrated by members of the Committee.) The programme is varied on the last Friday in February, when the Annual Festival is held at which four sections of the Lectures are worked, and on the last Friday in June when at the "Preceptors' Festival" in the first half one of the three degree ceremonies, in rotation, is rehearsed and in the second half, the ceremony of Installation. The Preceptors' Festival provides an opportunity for Brethren from the various recognised Lodges of Instruction, many of whom may never have met each other before the evening, to come together and work the ceremonies as a "scratch team", thereby demonstrating the universal nature of Emulation working.

Except on the evenings when the two Festivals are held, the Brethren attending pay dues by purchasing a plastic disc, which is collected later. Members pay 10 pence and receive a white disc; visitors pay 50 pence for a red disc.

In former times, though these days hardly ever, because of falling attendances and the introduction of the Installation into the cycle of ceremonies, a Brother aspiring to work a particular degree in the Chair, having had his name put down on the list, was eventually called as Candidate for that degree and worked his way in the succeeding weeks through the offices of Inner Guard, Junior Deacon, Senior Deacon, Junior Warden and Senior Warden, until six weeks later he took the Chair for that ceremony. At various points in the proceedings on a Friday evening the procedure continues to reflect the ideal, rather than the actual, state of affairs.

On a normal Friday (that is, except on the occasion of the Annual Festival), after the members of the precepting Committee have entered and made their way to the dais, the Officers for the evening put on their collars, and the Preceptor for the first half of the evening tells the Brethren to be seated. The Brother acting as Inner Guard should go at this point to the door and lock it. At this stage any vacancies among the Officers are filled by the Preceptor inviting Brethren to occupy the chairs or act as the particular Officer as the case may be. (If the Inner Guard is one of those appointed at this point, the Brother concerned should not forget to go to the door and lock it.)

The Lodge is then opened straightaway in all three degrees (the Brethren do not sit between the degrees) and is then resumed in the first degree if the work for the first part of the evening is the first or second degree, or in the second if the ceremony of Raising or the Installation is to be worked. At this point there will be a report and the Secretary or Assistant Secretary, who will have remained outside while the Lodge was opened to see to the reception of any latecomers, will be admitted (with the latecomers).

After a short pause, the Master will announce: "Brethren, the ceremony for rehearsal this evening is that of Initiation/Passing/Raising/Installation and Bro. .... will act as Candidate [or Master Elect]" At this point, the Brother called will stand. (Again for the sake of historical completeness, formerly if the Brother called were absent, the Master, prompted by the member of the Committee acting as Preceptor, would after a short pause announce: "Brother ....", giving the name of the next Brother on the list down to work the ceremony. If that Brother should also be absent, the process was repeated until a Candidate was found.) The Brother expecting to be called as Candidate for one of the three degrees should have positioned himself at the west end of the front row on the north side of the Lodge. The Brother due to act as Master Elect when the Installation is to be rehearsed should occupy a seat in the front row just to the east of the Secretary's table.

If the ceremony to be worked is the first degree, the Candidate, having stood, immediately makes his way to the edge of the floor in front of the Inner Guard, salutes and goes to the door, preceded by the Inner Guard. After a short pause the Tyler gives the knocks on the door and the ceremony proceeds. In the other two degrees the appropriate Deacon collects the Candidate and leads him to the edge of the floor in front of the Inner Guard for the test questions, and the ceremony proceeds. For the Installation the member of the Committee acting as Preceptor leads the Master Elect to the midline of the Lodge and presents him for Installation.

Each of the ceremonies proceeds in the manner already described earlier in Part II. The following matters, however, should be noted as peculiar to Emulation Lodge of Improvement:

(a) The Brother acting as Candidate is not prepared by the Tyler in any of the degrees. In the first degree, the Junior Deacon must therefore mime the removal of the imaginary h.w. and c.t..

(b) Similarly, in the first degree, the Master must mime the demonstration of the imaginary c.t..

(c) As the Candidate or Master Elect wears his Master Mason's or Installed Master's apron throughout the ceremony, the Senior Warden or Installing Master must mime the investiture with the apron.

(d) In the ceremony of passing, when the Master leaves his pedestal to deliver the explanation of the Tracing Board, the member of the Committee acting as Preceptor says, "Gather round, Brethren". It is the responsibility of one of the members of the Committee to gavel at the Master's pedestal at the words "...letter G.".

(e) In the ceremony of Raising, when the Deacons and Inner Guard go to the door to admit the Candidate, the member of the Committee acting as Preceptor says, "Brethren, it is at this point in a regular Lodge that the lights would be lowered." When the Candidate retires to restore himself, he says, "Brethren, it is at this point in a regular Lodge that the lights would be restored."

(f) In the ceremony of Installation when the Master Elect's attention is directed to the Secretary for the Ancient Charges and Regulations, the member of the Committee acting as Preceptor says "The first and the last, if you please, Brother Secretary."

(g) In the ceremony of Installation before the Lodge is resumed in the third degree, the Installing Master announces "Brethren, it is at this stage in a regular Lodge that Fellow Crafts would be asked to withdraw."

At the conclusion of the rehearsal, all the Brethren say, "Thank you, Worshipful Master", or "Thank you, Brother Installing Master" as the case may be.

As soon as the ceremony has been completed, the Master resumes the Lodge in the third degree (except when the ceremony has been that of Raising or Installation), and announces, "Brother Deacons, the dues". The Deacons then collect the discs that were issued earlier; the Senior Deacon starts with the member of the Committee acting as Preceptor and collects from the Brethren up to and including the Senior Warden; the Junior Deacon collects from the Inner Guard up to the Master. The Deacons take the bags with the discs to the Secretary, who after a brief check announces, "Worshipful Master, the dues will suffice" or "Worshipful Master, the dues are correct." Occasionally a member has forgotten to obtain a disc, or has arrived so late that the Secretary or Assistant Secretary has already entered the Lodge; in such a case he is expected to put his ten pence into the Deacon's bag, and the Secretary, by long custom announces, "Worshipful Master, the dues will *more than* suffice."

It is at this point that the Secretary will make any announcement that may need to be made, and it is at this point in the first meeting in January of each year that the Committee and Officers are elected.

The Worshipful Master then calls off the Lodge, and the Brethren (Officers having removed their collars) are free to leave the room for a short break while the Tyler changes, puts out or removes the Tracing Board.

The usual signal for the Brethren to return to the Lodge Room is a single knock given at the Junior Warden's pedestal by the member of the Committee acting as Preceptor for the second part. The Lodge is then called on.

The Minutes of the previous meeting are then taken, the customary formula in Emulation Lodge of Improvement being for the Master to ask, "Brother Secretary, are the Minutes ready?" at which the Secretary stands with step and sign, which he discharges, and reads the Minutes, concluding with the words, "Those are the Minutes, as recorded, Worshipful Master." At the end, the Master says, "Brethren, the Minutes of the last meeting are before you; all those who deem them a correct record and worthy of confirmation will signify the same in the manner usually observed among Masons. [after a pause] To the contrary? [after a pause] Brother Secretary," [the Secretary rises with step and sign] the Minutes are confirmed." The Secretary may reply: "Thank you, Worshipful Master." Small variations in the above wording (e.g. some Brethren prefer to say "On the contrary") are permissible as the Minutes are a matter of procedure rather than of ritual. In Emulation Lodge of Improvement the Minutes are not brought to the Master for signature.

If it appears from the Minutes that at the previous meeting one or more Brethren were proposed for joining, the Master then announces, "Brother Deacons, there is a ballot." The procedure for the ballot has been described in Chapter 6 and Chapter 15, but in Emulation Lodge of Improvement at the declaration of the ballot the form used is "Brethren, the ballot is in favour of Bro. ..." [or "the Candidates"]; "we shall be pleased to see him/them here as often as he/they can make it convenient to attend."

Next, the Master rises for the first time. The Secretary then reads out any applications for joining, at the end of which the Preceptor asks, without rising from his seat, "Are there any other propositions, Brethren?" If there are no applications, the Preceptor asks, "Are there any propositions, Brethren?"

The work of the second part of the evening is then demonstrated, at the end of which the Master rises for the second time. It should be noted that the risings are conducted in the third degree, except when the work has included the ceremony of Installation, in which case the Lodge will have been closed in the third and second degrees in the course of the ceremony.

As soon as the Master has sat after rising, the Preceptor says, from his seat, "The fourth by-law, if you please, Brother Secretary." The Secretary stands with step and sign and reads the by-law ("That no Brother shall be eligible to be elected to the Office of Master unless he is fully acquainted with the method of opening and closing the Lodge in the three Degrees, and of working the Ceremony intended for the occasion on which he is to preside, agreeably to the recognised system of this Lodge. That this By-Law be read by the Secretary at each meeting, immediately before the election of

Master."). Once the Secretary has resumed his seat, the Preceptor stands with step and sign, says, "Worshipful Master, I propose that Bro. Senior Warden occupy the Chair at our next meeting," [or "on Friday evening next"] and sits. The second member of the Committee seconds with the formula "Worshipful Master, I second." After the vote ("Brethren, the proposition is before you. Those in favour ... To the contrary.") the Master announces, "Brother Senior Warden," [The Senior Warden stands with step and sign] "you have been elected to occupy this chair on Friday evening next; you will appoint your Officers and name the work."

The Senior Warden replies, "Worshipful Master and Brethren, I thank you," discharges the sign and sits. He then appoints his Officers as follows: "Brother Junior Warden," [the Junior Warden stands with step and sign] "will you occupy this chair on Friday evening next?", to which the reply is, "With pleasure, Brother Master Elect." The Senior Warden proceeds, "Brother Senior Deacon, will you occupy the Junior Warden's chair?" (The Senior Deacon and the remaining Officers adopt the same procedure as the Junior Warden.) "Brother Junior Deacon, will you act as Senior Deacon? ... Brother Inner Guard, will you act as Junior Deacon?... Brother Candidate, will you act as Inner Guard?... The work will be the First ceremony and Charge/Second Ceremony and Tracing Board/Third Ceremony/Ceremony of Installation and Section...of the... Lecture/Ceremony of Installation."

The Master rises for the third time and the Preceptor rises with step and sign, "Hearty good wishes, Worshipful Master."

The Lodge is then closed in full and the Brethren retire.

PART III

Chapter 20

The Chaplain

The office of Chaplain, like the other additional offices permitted by Rule 104 of the Book of Constitutions, is one not contemplated in the basic scheme of Emulation Lodge of Improvement.

It may be as well to comment at once on two views that are often advanced on the Chaplain and his duties. The first is that no one but a clergyman should be appointed to the office. Now while it may be highly desirable that if a Lodge has a clergyman among its members it should be he who occupies the office of Chaplain, it does not follow that if there is no such member the office should be left vacant. If no Chaplain is appointed, it falls to the Master to deliver the prayers and it is only rarely that he will be in holy orders – so that a layman will still end up doing the work that might otherwise have fallen to the Chaplain!

The second view with which I would take issue is that the Chaplain should never deliver the prayers from memory, but should always read them. The basis for the view appears to be that as the prayers are addressed to the Almighty they should be rendered with the highest degree of accuracy, without the slightest risk of error. I would agree that the prayers, as much as other parts of the ritual, deserve to be delivered as accurately as possible, but provided the Chaplain can be relied on to get the sense of the prayers right, and not to produce nonsense, total accuracy is not essential: Masonic ceremonies are not a form of magic that will fail altogether of its effect if there is even the minutest departure from the appointed wording, and this is as true of the prayers as other parts of the ritual. (There is a very different sense in which Masonic ceremonies can be magic. Just occasionally the same electric atmosphere as builds up in a musical or dramatic performance when a special *rapport* is created between all those present – both performers and audience – arises at a Lodge meeting: "You could have heard a pin drop while the Master delivered the Charge". Such moments are spontaneous and cannot be contrived, but one of the aims of this book is to help create the conditions under which they are most likely to happen, by enabling the Master and his Officers to get the words and actions of the ceremonies right so that they can concentrate on putting across their meaning and the special lessons that the Masonic ritual sets out to teach.)

It follows from the above that the Brother appointed as Chaplain must be reliable and competent in the ritual. He must also possess a certain dignity of manner: prayers to the Deity must sound, as well as be, sincere. The office of Chaplain is frequently held by a senior member of a Lodge who has been "pensioned off" from a more active office, such as that of Secretary of Director of Ceremonies. Such Brethren most often fulfil all the criteria I have just mentioned, but some unfortunately no longer do so.

The duties of the Chaplain are fairly obvious, namely to deliver the various prayers, allocated in Emulation Working to the Master, which occur during the ceremonies of opening and closing the Lodge in the various degrees, and of the degrees themselves. The only matter of any difficulty is to ensure that the handover from the Master to the Chaplain in the openings and closings is effected smoothly. As there is no Chaplain in Emulation, there is no "correct" point for the "baton change", and it is a matter of common sense, not of ritual, but it is surprising how often an unnecessary hiatus occurs. The only advice which I can reasonably give in this book is that the Master and the Chaplain should agree a common policy between them in advance, and not leave matters to chance.

The Chaplain will normally have one further duty to perform: it will fall to him to say Grace before and after dinner.

Chapter 21

The Director of Ceremonies

Whole books have been written for, and about the duties of, the Director of Ceremonies. In one sense this is one of them. There is no doubt that such an Officer is useful for dealing with certain of the procedures which are met with in the average Lodge meeting, but the fact that Emulation Lodge of Improvement functions perfectly well without one is a clear indication that the Director of Ceremonies is not an indispensable Officer.

In most Lodges the Director of Ceremonies undertakes much of the work in the ceremony of Installation carried out in Emulation Lodge of Improvement by the Installing Master (see Chapter 16). Because the Director of Ceremonies, unlike the Installing Master, carries a wand, he is likely to find it convenient during the investiture of the Officers to delegate to the Assistant Director of Ceremonies the duty of bringing to the Master's pedestal the collars, gavels, columns and wands. Apart from the Installation ceremony, his actual work during the ceremonies themselves is confined to escorting Brethren who are carrying out a part of the work allocated to the Master and, usually, extinguishing and restoring the lights in the ceremony of raising. His rôle in the ceremonies of the three degrees is otherwise limited to directing or supervising the work and acting as a prompter for those who may need it (apart from the Master – who is the responsibility of the Immediate Past Master).

The other area for which the Director Ceremonies has responsibility within the Lodge Room is the management of the ceremonial, as distinct from the ceremonies (i.e. the ritual). This embraces the conducting of distinguished visitors into the Lodge, whether before or after it has been opened, leading the salutes to distinguished Brethren and – most notably – the organising of the processions into and out of the Lodge before it is opened and after it has been closed.

The manner of organising such processions can vary considerably from Lodge to Lodge, but one of the most common ways is as follows:

Before the Opening

The procession is formed in the ante-room in the order

ADC	DC
JD	SD
JW	SW
	WM

When it is time for the meeting to begin, the Director of Ceremonies leads the procession to the open door of the Lodge, steps forward, and calls "To order, Brethren, to receive the Worshipful Master and his Wardens." (If, for some reason, the Master is absent and a substitute takes his place, the correct form of the announcement is "To order, Brethren, to receive the acting Master and the Wardens." If one, or even both, of the Wardens is a substitute, no variation in the announcement is made on that account. Similar considerations apply to the announcement for the outgoing procession.) He may knock on the door to attract attention before he does so, but it is better if he does not; a good Director of Ceremonies should be able to command the attention of the Brethren by the crispness with which he makes announcements.

Having checked that the others have closed up on him, he sets off, leading the way at a dignified pace to the north side of the Master's pedestal. He should try to ensure that there is no straggling. The procession halts, and all turn inwards, the Deacons crossing their wands for the Master to pass beneath. The Director of Ceremonies "hands" the Master into his place, gives a court bow, steps back a short pace and turns right.

After a momentary pause for the Assistant Director of Ceremonies to draw level, he leads off again, halting at the east side of the Junior Warden's pedestal, where the procedure is repeated (except that the Senior Warden does not turn inwards). The procession makes its way to the south of the Senior Warden's pedestal, where the procedure is again repeated.

The Junior Deacon drops out immediately into his place and the rest of the procession moves off again. The Senior Deacon drops out at his place, and the Director of Ceremonies and Assistant Director of Ceremonies proceed together to their places. Each of these Officers, as he reaches his seat, places his wand in its stand.

After the Closing

At the start of the Closing Hymn the Assistant Director of Ceremonies sets off in a clockwise direction round the Lodge. During the first circuit, the Junior Deacon falls in behind him and then, as the procession reaches him, the Senior Deacon passes behind the Assistant Director of Ceremonies and in front of the Junior Deacon to take up his position on the latter's right. If the Assistant Director of Ceremonies has set the right pace it should not be necessary to halt or even slow down the procession as he does this. As the procession passes the Director of Ceremonies, he leaves his place and follows (rather than falls in) behind.

At the Junior Warden's pedestal the Director of Ceremonies "hands" the Junior Warden out, by the *west* side, into the procession, behind the Junior Deacon. He himself makes his way in an oblique line to the front of the Senior Warden's pedestal, where he "hands" out the Senior Warden, by the *north* side, in front of the Junior Warden and places him beside the latter, behind the Senior Deacon. Once again, these manoeuvres should be performed without halting or slowing the procession.

The Director of Ceremonies does not join the end of the procession, but proceeds alongside it, gradually overtaking it so that he arrives near the front of the Master's pedestal just as the Assistant Director of Ceremonies and Deacons pass it. The Assistant Director of Ceremonies leads the Deacons to a point roughly level with the Junior Warden's pedestal (depending on the size of the room) and halts; the Wardens halt just to the north of the Master's pedestal, facing south. If necessary the Director of Ceremonies restrains the Wardens with a discreet gesture, then "hands" out the Master by the *south* side and leads him to a position behind and between the Deacons. The Wardens should follow behind him and close up on the Master without any instruction or signal, but the Director of Ceremonies should be ready to signal to them if they seem disinclined to move.

The Director of Ceremonies collects the Grand Officers (if any), Past Grand Stewards (if any) and any others whom he intends to include in the procession, and places them behind the Wardens, seniors in front and to the right, as in this example:

ADC		[DC]
JD		SD
	WM	
JW		SW
GO		GO
SLGR		PGStwd
LGR		SLGR
LGR		LGR

Having formed the procession he proceeds to a position in front of the Master's pedestal and, facing west, announces "The Brethren will remain standing while the Worshipful Master, accompanied by his Wardens, the Grand Officers, Past Grand Stewards, holders of [Metropolitan Ranks,] [Provincial and District Grand Officers,] and Masters of other Lodges, retires from the Lodge."

He then takes his place at the head of the procession beside the Assistant Director of Ceremonies and says "Forward, Brethren." He leads the way to the north of the Senior Warden's pedestal, where he, the Assistant Director of Ceremonies and the Deacons turn inwards. The Deacons cross their wands while those in the procession pass beneath. When the last of them has done so, the Deacons lower their wands; the Director of Ceremonies, Assistant Director of Ceremonies and Deacons turn west, and bring up the rear of the procession, keeping neatly closed up.

It is worth noting that:

(a) If there are several members of a particular category scattered about the Lodge Room, the best way to collect them is to go to the most senior, call out, e.g. "Provincial Grand Officers", and lead the senior to his place in the procession, leaving the rest to find their own way. It is not necessary to include all the categories named, otherwise the procession can become too long. Indeed, a short procession is generally to be preferred to a long one, which is apt to straggle and become undignified.

(b) Metropolitan, Provincial and District Grand Masters are very senior Grand Officers in their own right, and take precedence accordingly.

(c) Other Provincial or District Grand Officers have no precedence as such outside their own Provinces or Districts, and the same applies to holders of Metropolitan ranks outside their Metropolitan Area.

(d) It is incorrect to refer to "reigning Masters". The correct term is "Masters of other Lodges".

From time to time a Lodge will receive a formal visit from the Metropolitan, Provincial or District Grand Master or one of his immediate hierarchy (often referred to as "chains" because their offices are senior enough to entitle them to wear chains when in performance of their official duties). Such a Brother will almost invariably bring his own Director of Ceremonies with him, who will organise his procession and lead his salute. The Director of Ceremonies of the Lodge will naturally act under his direction on such an occasion. Special protocol will apply for the visit, and the Lodge's Director of Ceremonies should be very wary of importing into ordinary meetings the features he will have witnessed then. In particular he should note that it is contrary to established protocol for anyone, however senior in rank, other than a "chain" to be placed beside the Master and in front of the Wardens in an outgoing procession. (By the same token, it is wrong for the new initiate to be placed beside the Master in the procession.)

The After-Proceedings

Although the Steward(s) will generally have the operational responsibility for the seating at the dinner or luncheon that follows a meeting, the Director of Ceremonies may well find himself called on to advise on the correct placement of members and visitors. Leaving aside special occasions, when the Lodge is likely to receive advice in this respect from the Metropolitan, Provincial or District Grand Secretary (or Director of Ceremonies), the Director of Ceremonies will need to be thoroughly familiar with the established practice of the Lodge, as well as the relative ranking of the Brethren present. He will also need to have some regard to the preferences of individual Brethren: in these days many Grand Officers neither expect nor wish to be seated on the top table, and unless there is a particularly compelling reason to do otherwise their wishes should be respected, especially if they are visitors and prefer to sit with their hosts. Finally, no Brother, *however senior*, must be allowed to sit between the Master and an initiate.

The modern tendency is towards the taking of wine at dinner being kept to a minimum, though many Lodges continue to maintain a long list of such informal toasts. In some Lodges the

Director of Ceremonies has charge of this; in others it is the responsibility of the Immediate Past Master and, except when the Master takes wine with the Immediate Past Master, the Director of Ceremonies is not directly involved; but he always has an advisory rôle. As a matter of principle, the Master should not take wine with anyone who will be the subject of a toast after dinner, and he should not call on the rest of the Brethren to take wine with an individual or class. The Director of Ceremonies should ensure that wine-taking is confined to the intervals between courses.

The basic procedure is for the Master to gavel (repeated by the Wardens), and for the Director of Ceremonies (or Immediate Past Master) to rise and announce "Brethren, the Worshipful Master will [be pleased to] take wine with his Wardens;" or "The Worshipful Master will [be pleased to] take wine with you all, and requests that you remain seated." At dinner, *only* the Master should use the Master's gavel. It is quite wrong for either the Director of Ceremonies or Immediate Past Master to gavel at any time; it is the Master who is presiding at dinner, and the gavel is the symbol of his authority there, just as it is in the Lodge.

The Director of Ceremonies should always be alert to ensure that the Master does not forget Grace at the end of the meal.

The current Toast Lists are usually distributed regularly by Metropolitan, Provincial or District authorities, but a sensible Director of Ceremonies will make sure that he and the Master are working from the most up-to-date version. During the toasts, it is a matter of personal preference (or the established custom of the Lodge) whether the Director of Ceremonies stands behind the chair of whoever is proposing, or replying to, the particular toast (calling for silence or claiming attention, as appropriate), or whether he leaves him to get on with it unaided; the former style while suitable at a well-attended dinner, may be inappropriate at a more intimate meal. Wherever he is situated while the toasts are being drunk, the Director of Ceremonies should be alive to the various pitfalls mentioned towards the end of Chapter 15.

If the Tyler does not dine with the Lodge, it usually falls to the Director of Ceremonies to propose the Tyler's toast. The correct form of the toast is set out in Chapter 4.

* * *

It must not be forgotten that the Director of Ceremonies has many responsibilities in relation to the preparations for the meetings of his Lodge. Even if he is not the Preceptor of the Lodge of Instruction (if any) sanctioned by the Lodge, he will usually have the task of conducting rehearsals before meetings and advising the Master on the customs and practices within the Lodge, as well as on the Brethren to whom the Master should depute those parts of the work that he does not wish to carry out himself, or whom he should invite to act in place of an absent Officer.

Chapter 22

The Almoner

The duties of the Almoner are entirely of a non-ceremonial nature, and therefore strictly fall outside the scope of this book. It may, however, be noted that whereas until 1975 the Almoner ranked immediately before the Organist (and from 1975 to 1991 after the Charity Steward), since that date he has ranked before the Charity Steward and the Deacons in recognition of the importance of his duties in looking after the welfare of Brethren and their dependants who may be in need of his assistance. Moreover, since 1991, although he is an additional Officer, his appointment has been mandatory. At first sight this may appear a contradiction in terms, as before that date it was of the essence of an additional Officer that his appointment was optional. In practice, however, it is a rather neat device that enables the holder of another office to be appointed Almoner as well, which is a significant benefit in a Lodge that has few – or few active – members.

Chapter 23

The Charity Steward

The duties of the Charity Steward, like those of the Almoner, are entirely of a non-ceremonial nature, and also fall outside the scope of this book.

It may, however, be noted that his office is of very recent creation, dating only from 1975, at which time he ranked after the Deacons and before the Almoner. Since 1991 he has ranked after the Almoner and before the Deacons. Like the Almoner he is an additional Officer whose appointment is mandatory, thus affording a rather typically English solution to the potential problem of filling the office in a Lodge with few members.

Chapter 24

The Assistant Director of Ceremonies

The office of Assistant Director of Ceremonies is in many cases a transitional one – either a training ground for the Brother who is earmarked for the office of Director of Ceremonies in a year or two's time, or a mentor's slot for the Brother who has just relinquished that Office to remain in, on hand to perform a function rather similar to that of the Immediate Past Master for his successor. This "hour glass" arrangement of inverting the holders of the two offices has much to commend it as it helps to ensure a smooth handover in the office of Director of Ceremonies.

The Assistant Director of Ceremonies does what the name of his office implies: he assists the Director of Ceremonies. In particular, during the investiture of Officers in the ceremony of Installation it is convenient if he undertakes the management of the collars, gavels, columns and wands, leaving the Director of Ceremonies free to conduct the Officers to and from the Master. He should not, however, forget that he may at any time be called on to deputise for him in his absence. He should therefore make himself thoroughly familiar with Chapter 21.

Chapter 25

The Organist

Music is one of the seven Liberal Arts and Sciences. There is no doubt that a skilled and sensitive musician can enormously enhance the ceremonies of a Lodge.

There is far more to the art of being a good Lodge Organist than might appear. A certain minimum (though not unduly demanding) level of competence on the organ or piano is essential, and if a Lodge cannot find a Brother who meets that level it is better to leave the office vacant. Almost more important, however, is the ability to shape discreet background music to the requirements of the perambulations and other parts of the ceremonies where no one is speaking.

When a tribute has been delivered to a departed member of the Lodge and the Brethren are standing to order in his memory, the Organist will sometimes play quietly at that point (the hymns "The Lord's my shepherd", "Abide with me" and "The day Thou gavest, Lord, is ended" are probably the most common). Some Brethren, however, feel strongly that complete silence should be observed at this point, and the Organist will be well advised, particularly if he is a visitor, to ascertain the custom of the Lodge beforehand from the Master and the Director of Ceremonies.

Many Organists see the investiture of the Officers in the ceremony of Installation as an opportunity to display their sense of humour. "I'll Walk Beside You" or "O for the Wings of a Dove" for a Deacon may be unexceptional, but "Writing Love Letters in the Sand" for the Secretary and "If I Were a Rich Man" for the Treasurer come into a different category. Subtlety has much to commend it.

In these days when Brethren capable of playing a keyboard instrument are increasingly hard to find, many Lodges rely on the services of a visitor who, either for love or for a fee, is willing to discharge the Organist's duties. It is perfectly proper for such a Brother to wear the Organist's collar while acting in the office. If he regularly acts as such, and the Lodge wishes to acknowledge his contribution by listing him on the summons, he must not, however, appear in the normal place in the list of Officers (Rule 104 of the Book of Constitutions precludes a Brother who is not a subscribing member from holding any office in the Lodge except that of Tyler), but should be placed below the Tyler and be described as "Acting Organist" or "Visiting Organist". Similarly he may not be invested in the office during the ceremony of Installation, though there can be no objection to the Master asking the Director of Ceremonies to conduct him to him at the end of the Installation and entrusting (but not investing) him with the collar with a few appropriate words.

It is a matter of personal choice whether the Organist plays music while waiting for the start of the meeting, but he will be expected to play suitable processional music when the Master enters with his Officers (and when he retires in procession at the end of the meeting) and to accompany the singing of "So mote it be" at the end of prayers, not to mention the Opening and Closing Hymns, as well as the National Anthem if it is sung either in the Lodge Room or at table after dinner. If the Lodge sings Grace before or after dinner or has other songs that are customarily used during after proceedings, the Organist will have even more duties to perform!

Chapter 26

The Assistant Secretary

The Assistant Secretary is the only one of the additional Officers who is appointed in Emulation Lodge of Improvement – and a very necessary appointment it is too!

His job there, as it is in any Lodge, is to relieve the Secretary of part of the burden of his very demanding office and, in the event of his absence, to stand in for him. In a regular Lodge it will be a matter for agreement between the Secretary and the Assistant Secretary how the duties are to be divided.

The office of Assistant Secretary, like that of Assistant Director of Ceremonies, is often a transitional one. The only useful guidance that I can offer its occupant is that he make himself familiar with Chapter 9.

Chapter 27

The Stewards

The Office of Steward is generally the first to be held by a Brother (and in these days quite often even before he has been raised). The primary duty of the Stewards is to serve wine at dinner, though in some Lodges, they are expected to serve the meal as well, and even in some cases to cook it. Such duties – particularly the last – are well outside the scope of this book.

It is usual for the most senior of the Stewards appointed, often, but quite incorrectly, referred to as the Senior Steward (no such office is recognised in the Book of Constitutions), to be a Past Master and for him to undertake the ordering of the meal and generally to attend to the correct seating of the Brethren at it. It is generally accepted that it is a part of the remaining Stewards' duties to make themselves familiar with the ritual work so that they may be able to stand in if one of the more senior Officers on the "ladder" should be absent. There is no doubt that it is a most useful discipline for junior Brethren to start as early as possible to familiarise themselves with the work.

I hope that this guide will prove helpful to them.

Appendix 1

A Few Words...

English pronunciation is notoriously difficult and can sometimes stump even the best of us. The headmaster of my preparatory school used to tell the story of the foreigner who, having wrestled none too successfully with *though*, *through*, *thought*, *thorough* and *trough*, finally gave up and went home when he saw a placard outside a theatre which read:

> Noël Coward's
> **CAVALCADE**
> "Pronounced success!"

I set out below a list, by no means exhaustive, of some words known to cause difficulty.

Adoniram	2nd Lecture, 5th Section	Ado<u>nigh</u>ram
artificer	3rd Degree; 2nd Lecture, 5th Section	ar<u>tiff</u>icer; NOT artissifer
bade	1st Lecture, 7th Section	bad (to rhyme with *mad*, not *made*)
Calimachus	2nd Lecture, 4th Section	Ca<u>limm</u>akus
composite	2nd Degree	<u>com</u>pozit; not compo<u>sight</u>
contrariety	1st Lecture, 5th Section	contrar<u>eye</u>-ety (as in *variety*)
defect	2nd Degree	de<u>fect</u>; not <u>dee</u>fect
Deity	1st Lecture, 4th and 7th Sections	D<u>ee</u>ity; rather than D<u>ay</u>ity
dictates	1st Lecture, 5th Section	<u>dict</u>ates
discharge	1st Degree	dis<u>charge</u>

excess	1st Lecture, 6th Section	ex<u>cess</u>
executers	2nd Lecture, 5th Section	exe<u>cue</u>ters; not ex<u>e</u>cutors
expatiate	1st Lecture, 1st Section	ex<u>pay</u>shiate
extant	2nd Lecture, 5th Section	<u>ex</u>tant
ethereal	1st Lecture, 4th Section	eth<u>ee</u>re-al
fiat	3rd Degree; 1st Lecture, 7th Section	f<u>ie</u>-at
grave	2nd Lecture, 4th Section *only*	gr<u>ah</u>ve (all other instances are as normal)
heinousness	3rd Degree	h<u>ay</u>nusness; not h<u>ee</u>nusness
impious	3rd Degree	<u>imp</u>yous; not imp<u>ie</u>-ous
indolence	3rd Lecture, 3rd Section	<u>in</u>dolence
Jehoshaphat	1st Lecture, 5th Section	Jeh<u>o</u>shafat
Marcellus	1st Lecture, 7th Section	Mar<u>sell</u>us; though Mar<u>chell</u>us and Mar<u>kell</u>us are not wrong
Menatschin	3rd Degree	Men<u>at</u>shin
Mesopotamia	1st Lecture, 4th Section	Mesopot<u>ay</u>mia
metopes	2nd Lecture, 4th Section	metop<u>ee</u>s
modillions	2nd Lecture, 4th Section	mod<u>ill</u>ions
molestation	2nd Degree	m<u>oh</u>lestation
mutules	2nd Lecture, 4th Section	m<u>oo</u>tyewls
Padan-aram	1st Lecture, 4th Section	P<u>ay</u>dan-<u>a</u>ram (as in *Arab*)
parallelopipedon	1st Lecture, 3rd Section	paral<u>le</u>lopipedon (short i as in *pip*)
pomegranates	2nd Degree	<u>pom</u>magranits; not pommiegranits or pom-granits
premise (verb)	1st Degree	prem<u>ize</u>
premises (noun)	2nd Lecture, 4th Section	<u>prem</u>isses
purport (noun)	1st Lecture, 6th Section	<u>pur</u>port
recesses	2nd Lecture, 4th Section	re<u>ses</u>ses
recourse	2nd Degree	re<u>course</u>
researches	2nd Degree; 3rd Degree	re<u>sear</u>ches
skirret	3rd Degree	do not confuse with *skillet* (a cooking pan)
specie	2nd Degree	sp<u>ee</u>shee

superficies	2nd Lecture, 2nd Section	super<u>fee</u>shees
tenet	Installation	t<u>ee</u>net or tenet
triglyphs	2nd Lecture, 4th Section	<u>try</u>gliffs
variegated	1st Lecture, 5th Section	va<u>iri</u>agated
volute	2nd Lecture, 4th Section	vo<u>lute</u>

Appendix 2

The Immortal Memory...

For some people remembering words seems to be easy. Most of us find that it takes some effort. Older generations (including mine) had to learn poetry and passages of Shakespeare at school, and we probably did it – at least to start with – "parrot-fashion", that is, by rote. Educational methods have changed over the years and many younger readers will not have had that grounding. On the other hand, memorising things seems to get harder as we get older, so perhaps younger Brethren still have the advantage of those of us who have had more practice!

In a short appendix I cannot hope to do more than point out a few strategies that may help both older and younger readers in the task of memorising and recalling the words of the Ritual. As a general observation, however, it cannot be stressed too much that no one who cannot render at least the sense of the words of the Ritual with reasonable fluency will be fully able to put across the ceremonies, and the important lessons they set out to teach, to a candidate. A Master, or more junior Officer, who does not have to worry about getting more or less the right words out is able to concentrate on putting across their meaning and will, moreover, gain a great deal in confidence from the knowledge that he has the words at his command.

The most important thing is to allow plenty of time for the process of learning, and to have some appreciation of how long that process will take. No one who is not an expert in the techniques of memorising can hope to learn twenty pages of ritual to the required standard in, say, forty-eight hours.

Secondly, it is important to be familiar with and to understand what the words *mean* before starting to learn them. Without a feel for the shape of a passage of ritual, the message that is being conveyed and the key words and phrases, learning will be harder and will be a matter of learning the words parrot-fashion.

Thirdly, what fixes a passage in the memory is the effort of dragging it out again, rather than the mere repetition of the words. So it is important, when settling down with the book to do the hard work of learning, not to glance immediately at the book when a word or phrase proves elusive.

Fourthly, it is important not to bite off too much to learn at once. Some Brethren will try to learn a whole ceremony, or at least a sizeable chunk, as a single unit. It is not uncommon to hear a Brother who is delivering, say, the Charge after Initiation, start very well indeed, but deteriorate more and more rapidly as he progresses. The reason will almost certainly be that each time he has settled down to learn it he has started at the beginning and has advanced as far as time and his concentration has permitted, so that the early part of the passage is considerably more familiar than the later parts. A useful strategy, therefore, is to start some learning sessions in the middle of the passage or, better still, with the final paragraph, progressing to the last two paragraphs, then the last three, and so on. It is an interesting psychological fact that most listeners will rate a ceremony that starts and finishes well more highly than one that tails off badly towards the end, even if the latter is overall the more accurate ceremony.

Fifthly, "easy come, easy go". Something that is learnt quickly over a short period will be forgotten equally quickly unless steps are taken to fix it in the memory. Periodically running over a passage at regular, though increasing, intervals will help in this process.

Sixthly, the use of mnemonics can be extraordinarily helpful. Several have been given in the main part of this book, but anyone can make up his own. Those with some familiarity with the history of the First World War will know of the nursing service, the

Voluntary Aid Detachment (VAD); this is a useful mnemonic for the Address to the Master in the Installation: "...and by *virtuous*, *amiable* and *discreet* conduct...". In many ways, moreover, the more abstruse a mnemonic is the more likely it is to stick in the mind.

* * *

Not everything will work for everyone, but the following method of learning which I use myself when learning a new passage of ritual may be helpful to some readers of this book:

1. I spend about a fortnight making myself familiar with the shape and meaning of the passage I am learning. I try to read it over once a day, preferably last thing at night before I turn out the light, so that it is swirling around in my subconscious as I am dropping off to sleep.

2. Once I feel comfortable with the passage, I settle down with the book for the hard slog of learning. I find that there is, unfortunately, no substitute for this. I try to get through this stage as quickly as possible.

3. Next comes the first part of the process of fixing, by dragging the words back out of my memory. I try to do this with the book handy for the shortest time possible.

4. Once I feel reasonably confident of being able to recall the words, I make use of "dead" time (while I am walking, for example) when I cannot do anything else that is useful, to run over the passage in my mind. Because in those circumstances I cannot keep referring to the book, I find this part of the process particularly effective in getting the words firmly into my memory.

5. Once I think I know the passage, I keep repeating the previous step until the words become almost second nature. Only then am I really able to deliver the passage under "real" conditions. Unfortunately it is not always possible to have

achieved this degree of polish before the passage has to be delivered.

6.   Thereafter it is a matter of continuing to apply the polish. I am sometimes asked how long it has taken me to learn a particular piece of ritual; if the piece is the Seventh Section of the First Lecture, my reply is: one week – and over thirty years. I was much younger when I originally learnt it and I doubt if I could manage the initial stages so quickly today! But it is the polish that I have applied over the succeeding years that really matters.